Early Intervention in Movement

Practical activities for early years settings

Christine Macintyre

David Fulton Publishers
London

David Fulton Publishers Ltd
Ormond House, 26-27 Boswell Street, London WC1N 3JZ

www.fultonpublishers.co.uk

First published in Great Britain in 2002 by David Fulton Publishers

British Library Cataloguing in Publication Data
A catalogue record for this book is available from the British Library.

ISBN 1-85346-870-3

Typeset by FiSH Books, London
Printed and bound in Great Britain by Bell & Bain Ltd, Glasgow

Contents

Acknowledgements

A great many thank yous are due to all those who have contributed to the compilation of this book. First, to all the children and their teachers who tried out the activities and lessons and evaluated them in terms of feasibility as well as developing movement abilities and skills. The teachers spoke of the children's gain in confidence as well as competence and thankfully the children said they had had fun.

Second, to the nursery nurses and classroom assistants who carried out meticulous observations and generously shared their findings and their analytical skills. They were tremendously enthusiastic, especially when they saw the difference their participation made to the programme, because it was obviously enriched by having more eyes that could see.

Thank you too, to the parents who allowed their children to participate both in the programme and in making the video, which allows others to appreciate the complexity of observing movement. Their initial doubts were overtaken by the children's enjoyment and willingness to continue. This was in no small measure attributable to the head teacher and her warmly supportive staff.

A special thank you to Anne Revels, an infant teacher in the Scottish Borders, who wrote the first poem and so started the whole thing off. Lastly to the Edinburgh University Media Staff for filming the children and helping to make them realise just how special they are.

The text has been brought to life by Mike Carter who composed the music for the rhymes and jingles. Thank you, Mike, for adding this magic music, I'm sure the children will enjoy it; especially if the teachers play and sing too!

Preface

This book is full of practical ideas to help lots of young children enjoy developing their movement abilities...and by lots that means children who move easily and skilfully, those who have movement learning difficulties and all of those who come between. Why is this so important? Quite apart from the special confidence that children gain from being able to participate in all sorts of activities at school and at home, the pervasive nature of movement means that inability in this aspect of development spills over into all other curriculum areas, especially those which depend on practical skills. Activities such as controlling a pencil in writing, manipulating number lines in maths, pouring and stirring, weighing and measuring in science, all depend on well-coordinated movement if they are to be efficiently done.

Especially in the Early Years, movement learning should be fun and free of stress: many of the activities in this text have rhymes and jingles as a stimulus, so introducing the language of movement to children alongside their actions (Department for Education and Employment (DfEE) 2000: 100). Most are developed into lesson plans to show how the learning outcomes within the activities fulfil the criteria set for physical development within the *Curriculum Guidance for the Foundation Stage* (DfEE 2000) and for expressive arts in the *5–14 Guidelines* (Scottish Office Education and Industry Department (SOEID) 1992). Some have music – specially written so that someone who can play just a little can try. The jingles can be sung by the adults and spoken by the children until, after several tries, they can sing too. The activities are based on experiences familiar to most Early Years children and so provide an easy route into further learning. The rhymes not only help movement memories and phonological awareness but also encourage listening skills. The expressive language used in many of the rhymes is important too, as it increases the dramatic effect of the activities; through extending the children's language, their imaginative storytelling and writing abilities are enhanced.

The rhymes can be used as a stimulus for discussion which allows children to share events in their lives. They may also promote understanding and empathy with others who have a different way of life. In this way physical activity can support other areas of learning in a different, less formal way.* The rhymes and activities may also be used at home by parents, thus providing invaluable extra practice.

In schools today, the increasing emphasis on inclusion means that many more children with movement learning difficulties will come into mainstream settings.* This means that all teachers will need to understand the nature of the children's difficulties, how they impact on learning across the curriculum and into the social life beyond it *and* how intervention can be planned to give most help.

The main thrust of this text is that simple but important movements should be done well so that they serve as useful building blocks for further development. The activities which are suggested have been tried out with different groups of children and so those who become involved in these programmes should gain confidence and competence in moving efficiently and effectively in different environments. I hope they do.

There are two other points to be made:

- * The asterisks indicate where direct links with *Curriculum Guidance for the Foundation Stage* and the *5–14 Guidelines* have been made.
- Throughout the text, the phrase 'the teachers' has been used to cover all those who share the responsibility of developing the learning of Early Years children. This is less cumbersome than writing 'teachers, nursery nurses, classroom assistants and parent helpers', although it is recognised that each will have different remits. I hope everyone finds this acceptable.

NB – A video showing a perceptual-motor programme in action, with comments from parents, the head teacher, classroom and special needs teachers and the children themselves (aged 6 and 7) is available from me, Dr Christine Macintyre, Faculty of Education, Edinburgh University, Holyrood Road, Edinburgh EH8 8AQ, £25.

Introduction

This text provides ideas for activity programmes which help all Early Years children to move better, i.e. more effectively and efficiently in many different environments. From the outset, some children will be 'natural' movers and appear both fleet of foot and dextrous. They will seek out challenges which allow them to go faster or higher, sometimes with little regard for their own safety. Perhaps they need to slow down and consider different ways of doing things or organising their resources so that they will stay safe. Another group of children cope, but at a lower level of competence and with little sense of enjoyment. Perhaps they need lots of safe and successful experiences so that they gain confidence in trying out new things and come to know that they can do them too. Then there are the children who find moving very difficult. Although many are bright and do well orally, they fluff even the simplest movement tasks and gain no pleasure from movement activities at all.

These are the children who used to be called 'clumsy'. Today they may be told that they have 'developmental coordination disorder' or 'dyspraxia' if they have had a specific diagnosis, and this would account for 8–10 per cent of all children, mainly boys. However, many more children with no label do not move easily and well. They have little awareness of how their bodies are functioning in space and their movement decisions, e.g. how fast to move and where to go, are miscued so that they soon find they can't do it, and avoid movement learning opportunities altogether. Very often children with dyslexia have a movement difficulty which hinders their articulation or their writing; children with Asperger Syndrome may also be helped by an exercise programme which stresses communication through movement. In fact at the present time, much more attention is being paid to the common difficulties, i.e. the comorbidity across the different syndromes, including autism and attention deficit hyperactivity disorder (ADHD). One of these is certainly movement. This perspective shows how all children can benefit from a regular movement programme, especially one which has been devised with all of these young people in mind.

Sometimes questions about maturation are asked, e.g. will the passage of time and increasing strength and longer limbs not be enough to overcome children's movement learning difficulties? For most children the answer is almost certainly 'No' (Dyspraxia Foundation 1999). Regular supervised and guided practice is the only way to ensure that all children fulfil their movement potential. After all no one would expect children to learn their sums without help, would they? Learning to move well needs expert help too. Another question often asked by teachers is, 'Are we supposed to be experts in this field too? Surely these are others – psychologists, physiotherapists and occupational therapists – who specialise in these difficulties?' While sympathy abounds, Keen (2001) explains that there has been an 80 per cent increase in the numbers of children referred for specialist help and the resources just won't stretch. And so it seems as if teachers, who are always anxious to do their best for all the children in their care, are going to have to cope.

Activity programmes which can help all children whether they have difficulties or not are one way forward. But before they can be implemented successfully, a number of questions have to be confronted to ensure that the intrinsic benefits and possible pitfalls are fully understood. Questions such as, What are these programmes called? What kinds of difficulties do children have? What is causing the problem? What sorts of activities have been shown to help? How have the children benefited? These are critically important questions which teachers, nursery nurses and possibly parents have to address, if this aspect of children's education is to be fully developed. Each question will now be discussed in turn.

What are these programmes called?

There are several names used to describe activity programmes, the two most usual being early intervention programmes and perceptual-motor programmes.

- Early intervention programmes – this term suggests that the timing of the input is critically important and that teachers, through helping the children develop their basic movement patterns, would be aiming to help them move at least as well as other children of the same age.
- Perceptual-motor programmes – this means that the activities would be based on developing the children's sensory integration, i.e. the way they perceive the environment and take instructions from it.

No matter what they are called, the focus or central aim is the same, i.e. that children should learn about movement and, in a safe environment, learn how to do it better. Why is this so important? Because movement is fundamental to all aspects of learning and to the developing self-confidence of young people. Being able to run, jump, ride a bike and play all sorts of games are the kinds of things children value. They count so much, for not being able to do them means being left out of games, never being chosen and often having a miserable time when one's friends go off to play. Moreover, not being able to do these activities is public – everyone can see – unlike inadequacies in classroom subjects, which can be discussed privately and hidden away.

Is movement, then, confined only to the hall or the playground? At first it might seem so, until one considers all the different kinds of movements that there are, for only then does the true range of activities which are dependent on movement become apparent. Even speaking clearly, or eating and drinking without difficulty, depend on coordinating the muscles in the mouth. Writing legibly, drawing, sewing, cooking – all these kinds of fine movements require coordination of the arms and hands. Then there are the gross motor activities, such as running and jumping, which depend on the coordination of the large muscle groups in the trunk and legs. All of these kinds of activities need to be mastered if children are to make the most of their time at home and at school (Figure 1).

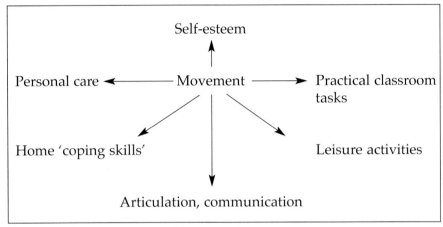

Figure 1 The pervasive influence of movement

There are several different kinds of movements, depending on the muscle groups which are called into play, but all of them depend on the children being able to

- take in (sensory) information from the environment accurately
- analyse it in the cerebral cortex of the brain and transmit the correct signals to the different muscle groups, then
- respond using the correct amount of strength, speed and space so that the movement is coordinated, rhythmical and balanced.

Parents and teachers who wish to help their children enjoy participating in lots of movement activities have to understand how this sequence of events interacts with the underlying movement abilities to produce skilled or less skilled movement. This is not easy, for movement is over in a flash. Observers must be able to analyse what is going on and either spot the level of challenge which would be appropriate to take the children's learning forward, or alternatively identify the cause of any difficulty. This would be essential in guiding decisions about intervention.

Then, of course, there is the 'other side' of moving well. This is the planning side – helping the children to know what to do, i.e. what kinds of movements they might make to fulfil a set task, or what kinds of movements might come logically together to produce a flowing sequence. Dighe and Kettles (1996) explain that some children 'may have great difficulty formulating an idea or conceptualising a plan of action. This can make it hard for them to reason through problems, even to know how to begin a task.'

What kinds of difficulties do children have?

And so, asking lots of questions such as 'What are you planning to do now?' or suggestions, e.g. 'I wonder if we could try…?', and basing interventions on the children's answers are the quite different kinds of interventions which are needed here.

Linked to planning is the organisation which is necessary if movement is to be efficient. Sometimes the children have only to organise their bodies to be ready to move; at other times they have other resources to order. Getting dressed and undressed is easy for many children, but organising the garments so that they go on in the correct order is totally baffling for others. Many children find it very difficult to order events, i.e. to appreciate the notions of 'now' and 'next'. This is apparent in any sequencing activity, e.g. following the theme in a story or being able to plan a piece of writing. It is important for observers to make accurate assessments of what is going on when children move: simply repeating technical instructions to achieve a better movement is no use if it is the underlying planning and organising which has caused the problem.

It can be seen then, that observing, analysing then intervening in children's movement needs skill, patience and practice. If they can't do it or get it wrong, the next question is to consider what is causing the problem.

What is causing the problem?

The problem could come from any of the sources already mentioned and shown in Figure 2.

But how would teachers know which aspect was faulty?

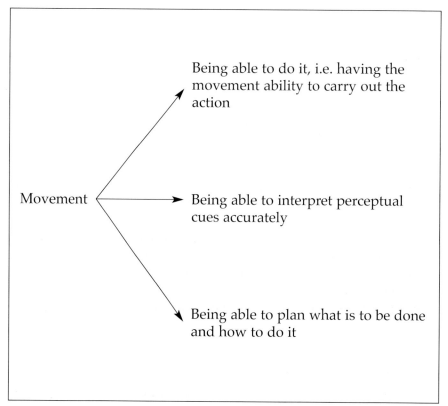

Figure 2 One movement analysis

'Being able to do it' difficulties

A 'being able to do it' difficulty could be shown in any of the following:

- lacking strength (if so, the child would appear floppy and seem to lack purpose)
- having too much strength (if so, the child would bump and barge and possibly break things)
- uncoordinated timing of the various components of different movements (if so, when attempting to catch a ball, the child might clutch at thin air after the ball had gone past)
- being unable to cross the midline of the body (if so, the child would be unable to draw a rainbow without changing hands at the top of the arc and would have great difficulty tying laces or fastening buttons or using a knife and fork)
- being unable to balance and so losing control (if so, the child would be likely to avoid any activity which took him or her off the ground).

Perceptual difficulties

On the other hand, a perceptual difficulty could be shown in:

- lacking concentration (if so, the child would be easily distracted by other things in the environment)
- being unable to track (if so, the child would have difficulty following the path of a ball or the words on a page)
- having difficulty in hearing instructions (if so, responses are likely to be delayed – possibly because the child is copying rather than reacting directly – or responses could be inappropriate due to the child misunderstanding the instructions)
- misjudging distances (if so, the child would drop things or knock into things)
- having poor body awareness (if so, the child would constantly be bumped and bruised).

Planning difficulties

Planning difficulties could be shown in:

- not knowing what to do (if so, the child would wander around looking lost or begin a task but without any sense of purpose)
- becoming agitated or unruly with lots of extra movements (if so, the child may be worried about asking instructions to be repeated)
- being able to do one task but not a subsequent one (if so, the child will begin readily, but wander off when other things have to be remembered)
- not being able to remember where the toilets are or even the way home.

Combined difficulties

To complicate things further, there are many shades and many different combinations of difficulties – one child may have just one while another has a whole range of problems. This makes accurate identification very tricky.

Observation and assessment

Teachers may find observation and assessment tantalising and frustrating: some children, having appeared to master a skill one day, forget it by the next, while others, who never seem to make any progress at all, will suddenly blossom and cope. This is why assessments, especially formal recorded assessments, should never rely on single observations made in only one environment, but be spaced out over several days covering different situations.

Therefore this text sets out

• to point out key features of the basic movement patterns which underpin them so that observers can readily spot what is amiss
• to provide observation schedules to help recording
• to confront some current issues, e.g. touching children, which impinge on what can be done
• to share some ideas for activities which have helped lots of children overcome difficulties.

Observing children moving to pinpoint what is wrong is quite complex, because (as already said) the three sources of difficulty, movement 'disabilities' and perceptual and planning difficulties, interact. Children are also likely to devise coping strategies to cover any inadequacy. Why is it important that this should not happen? Surely if they can cope, then that's fine? The trouble is that although they may compensate and appear to cope at a basic level, they are building their house upon the sand and won't manage when more demanding forms of coordination or balance are required. As movement is important for its own sake, across the curriculum and in all kinds of coping activities at home as well as in leisure pursuits, then early intervention and help are essential.

What sorts of activities have been shown to help?

In a perceptual-motor programme, the movements themselves are not complicated. Those who teach them aim to help the children to do their basic movement patterns well. To do this, the teachers and the children have to know what to do when and how to make adjustments which will be appropriate for different sorts of tasks – in other words they have to understand what movement is about. This focus on the basic movement patterns is made because these fundamental patterns are the stepping stones for all other kinds of movement. It is only the intention that varies. Even the most skilled footballer is dependent on being able to run well. The variation in direction and speed and size of steps is all built onto a basic running pattern.

What about competition?

Within the programmes, the only kind of competitive activity comes when the children aim to improve their own scores, e.g. 'Today I made four catches – that's one more than yesterday!' or when the teacher urges, 'Everyone try to hit the target three times before you sit on the bench'. This is because competing against each other suggests speed and this often takes away from the quality of the movements that are produced. In these programmes, the children learn to support each other, to take turns and to negotiate how activities should develop. In this way they learn to praise themselves and others through recognising effort as well as success. There is no 'weakest link'.

The text begins by analysing the basic movement patterns and giving suggestions for activities to help their development. Then the sensory input which guides perception is studied. Following that, sensitive issues such as touching children are discussed because these impinge upon what can be done. Finally, actual lesson plans which allow children 'to demonstrate their increasing competence in the basic movement patterns' and 'which use different kinds of movement with varied props' are described.* These experiences allow the children 'to express feelings and understand different emotional responses',* e.g. the puppet who is tied up with string but who longs to be free; the clown with baggy trousers and bright orange hair who makes everyone happy; children exploring the garden through the seasons and recognising the wildlife that lives there. All of these lessons provide a rich source for discussions and imaginative storytelling. Moreover, they are based on the criteria set by the national development groups and so teachers can be confident that the right sort of progress will be made.

How have the children benefited?

Most children who have taken part in perceptual-motor programmes over two school sessions have made significant gains in their ability to move well. As a result they have gained in confidence and have become more willing to try new things at home and at school. There have been movement gains, 'I can ride my bike, look at me!', social gains, 'I've got friends to play with now', and intellectual gains, 'I know the rules of that game and how to twist my hand to spin the hoop', but the most remarkable change has been in their self-esteem. Max summed it up (on the video, see Preface for details), when he said:

> I've always been nearly the biggest boy in my class you know and very soon I'm going to be the mostest fastest!

Teachers who have set up such programmes also have given the thumbs up, saying:

> It was a lot of work getting everything organised and arranging the programmes so that the children didn't miss out on other aspects of the curriculum, but I'm so glad that even the ones with really quite severe movement learning difficulties didn't go out of school for help. They've all come on well and no one has thought about them being different in any way. I was a bit nervous about the responsibility at first, but none of the activities are hard to plan and the children look forward to the daily programme. I just ask for a

higher level of performance from the able children without changing the content of the lesson too much. The children with ADHD have been calmer now that I have interspersed movement jingles at odd times in the day – just stretching and turning round and moving within the classroom seems to let the children focus on their work a bit more.

Parents too, despite initial doubts, have been very supportive:

When they asked if Tom could join in a daily movement programme, I was a bit concerned because I didn't want anyone to think he was stupid or different in any way. But when I saw how much encouragement he got and how he loved all the praise as well as being able to play football much better, I was delighted! In fact when they saw how much fun it was, all the other children wanted to go too. There was no sense that it was remedial in any way!

But of course there are children who take longer to make progress. Nonetheless, all of them can be helped. Their difficulties are summarised in Appendix 2 and further reading is listed in the Bibliography.

Chapter 1

Developing the basic movement patterns

This chapter will show how fun activities can be used to help develop skill in the basic movement patterns so that descriptions like 'awkward, clumsy and ungainly' are no longer appropriate. The movements themselves are simple, but doing them well gives the children a great deal of satisfaction; when they realise how much progress they have made, their confidence and self-esteem get a huge boost. And as all of this happens, it is vital that observers get time to see and to decide what kind of intervention would be the most helpful. Repeating the activities more than once allows time for this and also gives the children security in knowing that there is time to go at their own pace, there's no rush; in other words that practice in a calm atmosphere will improve their ability to do things well. The children also need time if they are to repeat and refine their movements* (DfEE 2000).

Instead of changing tasks, variety can come from

- varying the speed – fast, slow and very slow
- altering the direction – forwards, backwards and sideways
- adding obstacles – e.g. beanbags placed along the bench
- copying a partner – children of similar ability working together.

Most children love repetition just as they enjoy hearing the same stories and rhymes. Knowing when to suggest developments can be tricky. Often asking, 'Would you like to try...' gives the children the opportunity to say 'No', while the prompt, 'I know you can...' gives encouragement, especially if support can be offered for the first tries. Through this kind of gentle intervention, it is hoped that the children will be encouraged to practise and try more challenging activities when the time is right.

Many of the activities in this book include rhymes and jingles, because they are fun – especially for the youngest ones – and they help in both memorising the key features of the movement and the planning and organisation of what comes next. This helps sequencing, i.e. remembering the order of events. If rhymes are learned in the classroom, the children can concentrate on the movement patterns which accompany them when they come into the hall.

Analysing basic movement patterns

The analysis of each basic movement pattern is accompanied by a 'look for and correct' section, so that those who are less experienced in observing children moving have some pointers to help. There are lots more activities in the lesson plans in Chapter 4.

Most children will develop competence in their gross motor patterns first, but some can manage the fine ones while their gross patterns are still clumsy. It is best that teachers check them all and not make assumptions that because one set of movements is competent, the others are too.

Gross motor skills

This section describes various gross movements: being still, standing, walking, running, crawling and climbing, hopping, skipping, jumping and landing.

Being still

Teachers are often surprised and bemused by the question, 'Can the child stand still?' but even after reflection, they often admit they don't know. This seems strange until they realise that standing still – or sitting still – is something that children, especially those with movement difficulties, rarely do. There are several possible reasons:

- children find that keeping two sides of the body balanced is extremely difficult when they are still, because one set of muscles, stronger than the opposing set, is pulling them to one side
- children may have retained some primitive reflexes which prevent the body making more sophisticated movements
- children may be distracted by movements or sounds around them and not be able to resist investigating their source
- children may lack the concentration necessary to keep still.

For whatever reason, these children have to be on the move – for then they gain constant feedback from the environment and this is what keeps them feeling in control of their bodies. For some children, being still is a huge challenge and sometimes it just can't be met. If they are required to stand or sit for any length of time it is important that they have support, against a wall if standing or on a beanbag if sitting on the carpet. Desks and chairs must be such that the desks are at elbow height and the children's feet can rest securely, flat on the floor. With this kind of help they are freed to listen to instructions instead of having to use up energy and attention keeping their bodies still. 'Never being still' irritates other children, especially if they are nudged, *and* the teachers, who find they are distracted by the constant movement. Often the learning atmosphere is spoiled. This can cause the moving children to be scolded by their teacher and even to be rejected by their peer group. And yet staying still can be beyond the children's control. Everyone has to understand why and take steps to help.

Why should children learn to be still? Stability gives confidence which leads to competence in moving well.

Standing

It is important that children learn to stand well because then they are balanced and in control and can take a moment to think what it is they wish to do next. When they stand still, they can glean new information from the environment in terms of where they are in relation to other people and other things and this should allow them to plan their next movement from a secure base. This contrasts with being always on the move and making spatial decisions at the same time, with subsequent inappropriate amounts of strength and speed leading to awkward, clumsy movement. If children don't take time and make incorrect spatial judgements, they get bumped and bruised and sometimes they hurt others as well. This shakes any confidence they may have and makes them understandably reluctant to try again. Standing well also aids health, because breathing can be deeper and more refreshing if the body is held well (Photo 1). This is why learning and taking time to stand well should be part of every movement programme.

Standing well involves

- the body weight being evenly balanced on each foot
- balance being held with the feet together or fairly close
- the shoulders relaxing
- the arms tucking into the sides
- the neck being long
- the chin being held in naturally without stress.

Look for and correct

- Slumping, i.e. the rib cage down
- the shoulders held tense and high
- the head poked forward or held back
- the weight held unevenly on one foot
- the hips tilted or overextended back or forward.

Photo 1 Standing well

Standing well should be an integral part of any activity, as a well-poised start and finish helps develop a sense of body awareness, balance and control. If children find this difficult, getting them used to an instruction such as, 'Everybody standing well – 1, 2, 3' gives them time to adjust their position and think through, e.g. 'Where are my feet?' or 'Do I need to shift my weight?' or ' Is my head up high?' Sometimes in an effort to stand well, the children will show tension in their shoulders. If this happens, some easy swinging of the arms, maybe accompanied by a jingle, can help the children relax. 'Make a long neck like a swan – or a giraffe' can also be helpful advice.

Activities to help standing

As competent movement is rhythmical and flowing, it can be helpful to introduce all sorts of activities accompanied by rhymes. These can be said slowly at first and faster or slower as the children's skill improves. The rhyme can add to the fun and help the short-term memory too.

Pillars and Posts

Standing still and standing tall
Careful not to move at all,
Let the hoop pass slowly by,
Change over, let your partner try.

In twos, one child, i.e. the pillar, stands tall and still while the other tries to post a hoop over the child's head, down to the floor and up again without touching any part of the body. They then change over and try again. Once this has been done successfully, the children can increase or decrease the speed. The excitement may cause the pillar to jump up and down, so any increase in speed needs care, but in fact doing something slowly is often more difficult. The hoop can travel down, then up again – then it can be exchanged above head height to add more challenge and variety.

This simple activity means that the pillars have to keep their hands closely into their sides and hold their whole body still and tall for a moment or two. The passage of the hoop encourages the pillar to think about the position of shoulders, trunk, hips and legs as the hoop passes by. Children posting the hoop have to control the hoop as they stoop and stretch and they have to adjust to any movement the pillar makes. The hoop must be kept moving, but it can be very slowly so that the pillar has lots of challenge in keeping still. This activity develops both body and partner awareness. Later, a line of children can try passing the hoop on after each successful try. If a pillar is touched he or she has to call out, 'Stop!' and the challenge starts again.

Competent pillars can be encouraged to stand with their eyes closed but for most young children, this eyes-closed balance is too difficult.

Walking

Often a movement and subsequent learning difficulty can first be spotted through a child's gait. Any walking action which appears awkward or out of control after about age 2 needs to be corrected. Children need to walk well, i.e. using the correct amount of strength and speed to build up momentum, so that a rhythmical, efficient action can be established. Walking well is a progression from standing well; it is important in its own right and because it is the precursor of running and other more advanced skills such as dodging and marking.

Walking well involves all the components of standing well plus

- transferring the weight smoothly from one foot to the other
- sustaining a smooth and continuous action
- swinging the arms in opposition to help the momentum of the action
- keeping the toes and knees facing forwards.

Look for and correct

- A wide, side-to-side base
- any jerkiness possibly coming from an uneven stride pattern
- a stilted gait possibly due to the foot and arm on the same side going forward together
- toes turning in – and knees and hips, possibly due to lack of strength in the pelvic girdle; this badly affects walking and running as the free leg has to swing round the standing foot rather than pass through the space (Photo 2).
- the body 'heaving' along, legs appearing to trail, which may be due to poor muscle tone which allows the knees and toes to turn in.

Photo 2 Inefficient walking due to poor muscle tone

Activities to help walking
The first activity is walking along the lines on the gym floor, or freely if there are no lines.

A Walking Jingle

Smartly, smartly, walk so tall,
Hardly touch the ground at all,
Swinging arms and head held high.
Wave to a friend as you pass by.

Toes are forward, look and see,
Smile and walk so merrily,
Walking here and walking there,
Smartly walking everywhere.

A Walking Jingle

1. Smartly, smartly, walk so tall,
Hardly touch the ground at all,
Swinging arms and head held high.
Wave to a friend as you pass by.

2. Toes are forward, look and see,
Smile and walk so merrily,
Walking here and walking there,
Smartly walking everywhere.

The second activity is walking along the lines on the gym floor

- on outside of feet
- on tiptoes for a short distance
- heel to toe in a straight line.

NB Look for any extra curling action with the arms: if this occurs ask for physiotherapy as the child may not realise this is happening and won't be able to control it. It is a sign that the nerve impulses or messages from the brain are going to all four limbs instead of just two.

The third activity is walking quickly then stopping inside a hoop...all with control.

Equipment: coloured plastic hoops spread over the floor.

Children have a 'secret' colour which they have to find when it comes to 'Getting ready to...stop?' If the children find they have another child within the same hoop, then they have to 'stick together' for the next turn of walking. Moments of fun and body awareness training can happen if the children have to stick side to side or back to back or even in threes. This happens when teachers or their helpers gradually reduce the number of hoops on the floor so that there are fewer stations.

Marching

As a progression from walking activities, young children enjoy marching like soldiers. This encourages them to be strong and upright and count the steps as they go. They enjoy commands like 'Halt' or 'Right turn' or 'Stand easy' or 'Salute' – as long as all are presented in a fun way. Observers will find that this is a good activity for assessing body awareness, for as the children obey the command 'Salute', it will become apparent if they know where the sides of their heads are! This is also a useful way to introduce changes of direction, for some children find great difficulty in turning corners sharply and will take a curved path instead.

Marching squares

Equipment: canes to form squares or chalked lines or ropes laid out as a square (Figure 3).

For 3- and 4-year-olds
March forward smartly for 4 steps and 'wait, wait, wait'
March backwards for 4 steps and 'wait, wait, wait'
Repeat adding a clap on the wait
Teacher counts out rhythmically:

1, 2, 3, 4 and wait, wait, wait
Back 2, 3, 4 and wait, wait, wait
Forward 2, 3, 4 and clap, clap, clap
Back 2, 3, 4 and clap, clap, clap

Progression:

a)

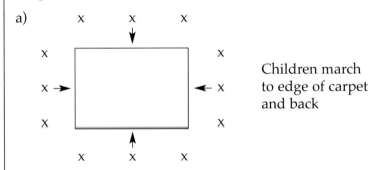

Children march to edge of carpet and back

HELPS

Rhythmical awareness

Control

Listening skills

Body awareness (marching tall, heads high)
Rhythm through counting to 4
Awareness of other children as they keep in line

Laterality (awareness of sidedness)

Figure 3 Marching squares

This activity is very good for spatial awareness, for the children have to keep in line with the other marchers – and for timing, as the marching and clapping rhythm keeps everyone together. The development of laterality, i.e. awareness of space to the side, is also helped. This competence is often slow to develop – many children will be 9 before they have it, but laterality is important in establishing hand dominance. It helps skills such as writing and reading, in fact any activity where moving to the side is important.

Walking and balancing on a bench
Equipment: bench, beanbags, basket, hoop.

Walking Along the Bench Jingle

Look at me, I can walk so straight and tall,
I go carefully, I don't fall!
My arms and hands are by my side,
To help me balance I hold them wide.
At the end of the bench I jump down – STAT
And land very safely on the mat!

In this activity it is a good idea to stress jumping down in a resilient way, i.e. knees bend and stretch up again to stand tall. This establishes the importance of safe landings and finishing a movement with control, rather than running off to the next activity. The children should walk along the bench confidently and well poised without looking down or wobbling before adding any other challenges. The arm movement should be controlled and not cause the body to overbalance.

The first part of the activity is stepping over beanbags placed on the bench (Photo 3).

Photo 3 Poised walking on a bench, stepping over beanbags

The second part is bending to gather up the beanbags, then tossing them into a basket while still standing on the end of the bench. This bending and lifting, then sustaining poise while throwing, adds quite a difficult balance challenge.

The third part is placing the beanbags in a hoop at the far end of the room (the children have then to retain more than one instruction, so helping their planning skills). The hoop can be red, green or blue if the class theme is colours, big, middle-sized or small if the theme concerns the concept of size. Children can even put the beanbag in the hoop on their right or left, if practices for hand dominance are required.

Often having a subsequent simple activity like this saves queuing at the bench; it is absolutely safe and so the teacher can concentrate on observing, correcting or supporting the child who is balancing. It is important to help the children to concentrate on their walking pattern, asking 'Can you feel where your feet go when you are looking up?' or saying 'Heel to toe' as the child goes along, in the hope that the transfer of weight will be felt – rather than sustaining a flat-footed action which never establishes momentum.

The fourth part of the activity is walking along a bench not touching obstacles which have been spaced out, e.g. a rope supported by skittles which are astride the bench, or a large hoop which the children have to climb through. In this activity, lifting one leg to step over quite a high obstacle can make balancing difficult. The child may need one hand lightly supported at first. Let the child go slowly till confidence is gained.

Finally, children can practise walking up and down an inclined bench keeping tall. This can be quite difficult for some children, so the incline should be slight at first. Benches or planks with different inclines can be added to a climbing frame, so providing different levels of challenge. Some children will enjoy climbing to retrieve a band from the frame which they wear as a trophy. Teachers can make sure there are plenty of bands hidden low down too.

Some children may prefer to crawl up the bench first holding on to the sides – but remember that some children can't crawl, so this isn't always a safer alternative way of travelling.

Stalking and prowling
Children enjoy stalking through the woods and all sorts of stalking games can be helpful in getting the children to concentrate on the heel–toe action of each foot. This is very good for body awareness and for leading into a running action, where the transfer of weight from heel to toe is important. It must be said, however, that the children usually crouch forward to control the placement of the foot on the floor, so this kind of activity should come only after a well-poised walking action is mastered.

Running

Running is walking quickly with the addition of a flight phase between each step. Many children attempt a flat-footed run at age 2, and some older ones retain this action and so lack the momentum which comes from the weight being transferred quickly from heel to toe and from one foot to the other. In the mature running pattern only the ball of the foot touches the ground.

Efficient running involves:

- showing a definite flight phase
- the body leaning slightly forward into the action
- the legs extending as they support the body weight (Photo 4)
- the stride pattern being long and regular
- arms punching forwards in opposition to the legs
- travelling at a fast speed.

Photo 4 Running

Look for and correct

- The pace being too slow to allow flight
- the arms swinging across the trunk
- feet going down flat
- the weight sinking the body into the ground rather than skimming over it
- the body twisting from side to side
- no arm action.

NB Avoid having races unless for the last moment or two in a lesson, for the children get excited; they are often noisy and this can upset some noise-sensitive children. Whenever speed is introduced, most children forget about the quality of what they are doing in the dash to be first. So speed is best kept until the action can be done well.

Activities to help running
Begin by having the children standing ready to run, i.e. with one foot ahead, leaning slightly forward, with arms held at 90 degrees.

A Running Jingle

Find a place to run to – go there fast
Get there very quickly, don't be last,
Take a little rest, then stand just so -
Are you ready,
Are you steady?
Off you go!

Children enjoy running and they want to 'go fast' but short spells across the hall are best. If there are children who find control difficult, then avoid having them run towards a wall or any obstacle which could harm them – try jogging interspersed with sprinting round the room. Again it is best to have brief spells with times for rests and regaining poise as suggested in the jingles.

Next, divide the children into three groups:

• Yellows: running on the spot
• Blues: jogging
• Reds: running fast

The teacher calls out:

Ready to change – Yellows – run, Reds – jog, Blues – on the spot

changing the order frequently so that brief spells of each kind of activity intermingle.

Changing colours like this means that there are fewer children running fast at once. Those who are have to avoid those that are on the spot and those who are jogging. The children enjoy listening for instructions which tell them when to change speed.

NB Running needs to have a purpose, but running combined with jumping needs quite sophisticated coordination and landings should be onto a mat until control is gained. Running while manipulating apparatus, e.g. a bat and ball, can be too difficult for many of the children in these programmes.

Simple activities like running to fetch a quoit (light and easy to carry) and then placing it over a stick or into a hoop at the other end of the hall seem like a real game, yet allow the children to concentrate on the running action and the direction in which they are travelling – without being confused by the coordination which is required when manipulating equipment is part of the activity.

Crawling and climbing

These two activities can be analysed together for basically they are the same action. This becomes evident if one pictures a child crawling or climbing upstairs. Although many children crawl and climb with ease and at amazing speed, others find this action impossible. Parents often think their child has missed a stage, i.e. missing out crawling and going straight to walking, when in fact the coordination in the action has been too difficult. This may be because myelination of the axons is as yet incomplete and this insulation which should help to convey nerve impulses directly along one path does not do its job, and they jump across to another. This means that messages to the muscles are confused or delayed: confused, if the instructions which should have gone to one limb have gone to all four leaving the child unable to move one arm or leg independently of the others, or delayed, if there is hesitation at the synapses, i.e. the spaces between the dendrites, which hampers the speed of the instruction getting through (Figure 4). This explains why some children delay for a moment or two before beginning a task. This hesitation should be recorded in any observation.

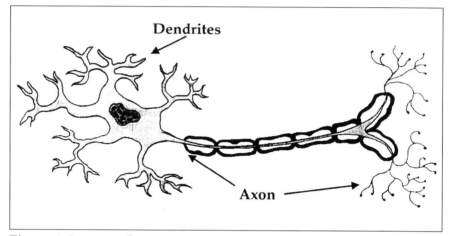

Figure 4 Axons and synapses

The importance of crawling

As the first form of real locomotion, being able to crawl opens up a whole new environment for the child to explore. Early judgements about distance, e.g. 'How far can I go?' and perspective, e.g. 'Can I get through the space between the chair and the table?' and direction, e.g. 'Where do I place my hands if I want to turn a corner?', are made when a carer is hovering, ready to come to the rescue. And so the learning horizons are opened up in a safe environment and the results of the explorations are stored away to inform later tries.

In addition, crawling also helps balance, perhaps a less obvious gain. Picture a child in the crawling position securely balanced on all four limbs. When the child reaches out to grasp an object, there has to be a shift of the child's weight so that three limbs sustain the balance. The stretch tells the child how far and in what direction the object is and as the arm comes back to the floor, the weight must be shifted again so that all four limbs sustain the balance. This shifting, i.e. losing and regaining balance, is essential practice for many more sophisticated activities and should not be missed. Crawling should form part of every activity programme. Teachers trying to help have to be sure they know which limb moves when (Photo 5).

Photo 5 Helping the crawling pattern (the teacher is alongside but not touching the child)

Activities to help crawling and climbing

In prone kneeling (the crawling position), the children should have a band in either hand. Stretch out one band and shake it (this means the children will watch their hand and track the direction it travels). **Change over hands.** Once they can adjust their balance in this activity, the band can slip over their shoe and they can do the same with each leg. Encourage the children to feel where the band goes, even when they don't see it. This can be a dog wagging its tail or a horse bucking.

Keeping the band in each hand, crawl across a mat and/or through a hoop to a line on the floor. If this is difficult, the teacher can call out 'Red band, blue band' to assist the sequence of the action.

Another activity is crawling through a tunnel (Photo 6). This is good fun for the children who can crawl and helps those who find it difficult, because the tunnel restricts where the limbs can go – this keeps the action contained and controlled.

Hopping

Hopping is fun but not over long distances as it is very tiring. Three hops building up to six hops is plenty. If children are asked to do more than that, e.g. to hop all the way across the hall, the body is liable to slump and the action becomes a huge, ungainly effort. This

Photo 6 Crawling through a tunnel

defeats any attempt to have poise, balance and control in the movement.

If the children have difficulty, asking them to stand feet apart, then gently to transfer their weight over to one leg while still keeping tall, then back to the other leg, can help the children feel the balance and therefore the correct position of the action. Once the transfer of weight is felt, then standing erect on one foot with the other tucked in so that it does not hinder the pumping action is the next step. If the children stand facing a support – wall bars are ideal – and hold on at chest height, it is often easier for them to feel the weight shift which helps the hopping action. They can look down to check the position of their foot to begin with, but in real hopping they should try to keep tall. Hopping is usually best taught before skipping is attempted. Children should try using both feet as this helps establish a sense of dominance...but only for a moment or two.

A Hopping Jingle

Hopping – hopping – on we go,
Sometimes high and sometimes low.
On my right foot one, two, three,
And on my left, I can, you see!
Feet together – have a rest,
We need to practise – what a pest – GRRRR
Now we can do it – we're the best!

Some children find interspersing running with hopping less demanding than hopping by itself, for the speed gained from running can provide the momentum for hopping. If this is the case, then it's a good idea to change the first lines of the jingle to

> Hopping and running – on we go,
> Sometimes fast and sometimes slow,
> Hopping on my right foot one, two, three,
> And on my left, I can, you see!

Activities to help hopping

This hop and pop activity needs hoops spread out over the floor. The children hop along a line and jump into a hoop (pop). They rest there till they see an empty hoop and go off again. If two children pop into the same hoop, they have to do the next sequence together.

A Hopping and Popping Jingle

> Hop, hop, hop, then pop i go,
> Sometimes high and sometimes low,
> Hopping along, then resting to see
> If anyone wants to come hopping with me!
>
> Now I have a friend and we go hop, hop, hop,
> It's really good fun, but soon we have to stop
> For our legs are tired and we're ready to flop,
> So we look for a hoop and in we pop!

In a progression activity, the children pop into the hoop, pick it up and hoop-la till the hoop falls to the floor. When this happens, they hop off again.

Skipping

Skipping is a step-hop with alternate feet leading. The action should be continuous and rhythmic. If children find this difficult, then count out the rhythm for them, 'Step, hop, step, hop', or have them say a jingle as they try. Holding hands so that a struggling child can feel the rhythm from the teacher, or another who can do it, is a good plan. The teacher as partner can add some elevation to the pattern to let the child feel the flight part of the action.

A Skipping Jingle

> Let's go skipping up and down,
> What a funny way to go into town,
> Our legs are pushing our heads up high,
> Look – we're nearly at the sky!
>
> Step – hop, step – hop, off we go,
> It's fun to skip like this you know!

Photo 7 Skipping

A good skipping action involves:

- the step being a rhythmical step-hop on alternate feet
- the knees being lifted up in front
- the body staying upright (Photo 7).

Look for and correct

- The same foot leading consecutive actions to give a galloping step
- the rhythm being uneven and the action jerky
- the step-hop being interspersed with a running action
- arms trying to lift the body, rather than the legs pushing strongly.

Activities to help skipping
If the children take giant steps – right foot, left foot – then they have to take time to transfer the body weight over the standing foot. Then add a hop. This action then becomes step-hop, step-hop. When this is established, reduce the size of the step and increase the speed.

Some children find it easier to begin with galloping, i.e. the same foot leading them round the room. Change after four counts. The teacher counts out:

1 and 2 and 3 and change and 1 and 2 and 3 and change, then

1 and 2 and 1 and 2 and 1 and 2 [i.e. changing each foot after two counts].

The best help is for someone who can do it to skip alongside someone who can't, taking hands so that the rhythm passes from one to the next.

Jumping

There are two kinds of jumping which have different aims and which make different demands on the body. These are

- jumping for distance, as in jumping over a puddle
- jumping for height, as in jumping up to catch a ball.

The first, i.e. jumping for distance, probably needs a single-foot take-off and the action is an extension of the running action – the jump just requiring an extra period of flight. Time in the air equals the distance gained. This is why running with giant steps, i.e. bounding, can be an effective practice. The landing may be on to one foot or two feet depending on whether the action is to be carried on or finishes with the landing.

In the second action, jumping for height, the take-off requires a sudden burst of strength upwards and two feet must leave the ground at once. The direction of the jump is up rather than forwards and the push happens just underneath the action rather than before it. The arms should help the take-off.

Jumping for distance involves all the components of running well plus

- identifying the take-off foot and using it consistently
- extending the push-off leg powerfully
- controlling the balance of the body in the flight phase
- using the arms to assist the momentum of the action
- releasing the power to land resiliently and safely.

Look for and correct

- an overlong run which confuses the take-off
- a flustered take-off (meaning that the child is not sure which foot is the take-off foot)
- the head poking forward trying to help the action but taking the body off balance
- eyes looking down so that the intention is down before up.

Activities to help jumping for distance

Figure 5 illustrates four stages in running and jumping.

Begin with a rope between two skittles but lying on the ground. Ask the children to run over the rope. This establishes the momentum. The children should repeat this several times so that they establish which is their leading foot. Only then should the rope be raised.

NB Avoid changing heights and directions at once. Adding height is easier as a continuous running action can be followed through. Once a change of direction is added, the transition may mean that there has to be adjustment of the feet and this may cause confusion as to which foot is the leading one.

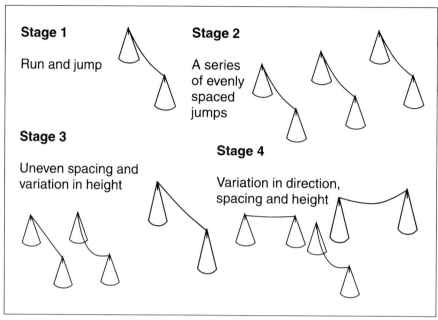

Figure 5 Stages in running and jumping

Activities to help jumping for height
Equipment: a rope stretched between netball stands with coloured bands suspended from it.

Children stand underneath and leap up to try to touch or catch the bands.

Most practices for jumping for height are combined with catching a ball and both the coordination and the timing can cause problems. This can be too difficult for many Early Years children although some will manage. Once the ball is introduced, concentrating on the jumping action becomes difficult.

Landing

It is important that children learn how to land safely, i.e. resiliently with the knees bending to absorb the body weight and so preventing jarring (Photo 8). This can be practised as jumping down from a low box (a bench is just too low and makes it hard to have time to adopt the correct position). The body should stay upright and it is important that the children learn how to sustain this balance, especially if there is a subsequent action.

Landing and rolling
Inevitably some children won't manage to land in a balanced way and even those who can do so need to be ready for times when greater challenges might cause them to be off balance. Landing and rolling is an alternative way for the body weight to continue the action without harm. If this is to happen, the sharp bits, i.e. elbows and knees, must be tucked in and the shoulders must be rounded to keep the head from banging down onto the mat.

Photo 8 Landing well

Practices
Have the children in prone kneeling, i.e. the crawling position. Then have them tuck one hand through the arch made by the other. They then let the head follow through and this takes the body into a safe roll. Emphasise keeping the elbows well tucked in. If they can then keep their backs rounded and sustain some momentum, they will be able to roll right round back into the original position. This can be a competition, 'Who can roll right round?' This is a good preparation for the forward roll, because awareness of the back being rounded has been established.

Forward Roll
This can be practised as an activity on its own; it is something children like to say they can do. It provides a good opportunity for the teacher to see who has awareness of all their body parts, i.e. who can round the back and keep balanced throughout the roll. Adult supervision is essential till the children are able to keep their arms strong and let their heads be tucked in safely. Only the back of the head should touch the mat.

Rolling should be practised in a variety of ways, from lying stretched out (a pencil roll), from a crawling position, then from kneeling (sideways rolls). The aim is that if the children fall they automatically tuck in all the sharp parts and leave the padded parts, i.e. the back of the shoulders and the hips, to take the weight. Rolling is really a safety mechanism. Older children may use it as transition, to join together two other movements into a sequence.

Manipulative skills

This section describes the skills of throwing and catching.

Throwing

Many children, especially boys, throw with power and accuracy while others find it an extraordinarily difficult thing to do. In the early years, it is often the release of the ball, i.e. the letting go, which causes most difficulty. The coordination required in letting go causes lots of problems. So lots of practices of rolling a ball are good precursors of throwing because the hand action is the same – the moment of release just happens lower down.

Once the release has been practised, then the stance must be checked. The hand holding the ball has to have a clear pathway so the leg on that side of the body must be out of the way to allow the arm to swing through.

Activities to help underarm throwing

Any kind of bowling into a basket or knocking down skittles lets children practise releasing the ball at the right time and establishes the feel and pattern of the follow through. This preliminary practice prevents catchers getting frustrated when the ball, released by the thrower too soon or too late, goes off in the wrong direction.

Teachers should check the stance – opposite foot to the bowling/throwing arm forward. With the older children it is helpful to stress the rocking action from back to front foot; this really is the transfer of weight which helps to propel a throw. The coordination involved in overarm throwing is too complex for most children at this stage, although some will do it naturally. It would not be appropriate to teach it to a group.

Catching

Catching requires the children to make a number of estimations, e.g. the pace and direction of the flight path of the ball. Children with poor tracking skills and a poor sense of timing find it difficult. The best idea is to use a large, soft ball which drops rather than runs away or most time will be spent chasing it. This kind of ball travels slightly slower and above all it doesn't hurt when mistimings mean bumped noses.

The space between catcher and thrower is important; if the children stand too close then there is not time to make any adjustment in where to receive the ball; on the other hand if the distance is too great, the thrower is likely to overestimate the strength that is needed and throw wildly.

NB Children who are field dependent, i.e. who have difficulty seeing objects standing out from their background (rather like having no three-dimensional sight), won't see the approaching ball till later than the other children. This means that they have a shorter spell in which to move to the correct spot to receive the ball or to place their basket appropriately. Children who clutch thin air too late to catch the ball may have this visual difficulty. A brightly coloured ball which stands out can help.

Secure catching involves

- keeping an eye on the ball (tracking)
- allowing the speed of the ball to be absorbed by the body
- having two hands placed appropriately, making a basket.

Look for and correct

- tense arms and hands
- looking away from the oncoming ball
- closing hands too early or too late
- shutting eyes or turning away from the oncoming ball (avoidance action).

If children have difficulties, it can sometimes help to stand behind them and hold their hands to let them feel the correct timing of the action.

This section describes aspects of the fine motor skills of writing, cutting, playing the piano, drawing, moulding, threading and pincer grip activities. There are many fine motor skills which depend on coordination, balance and the correct application of strength and speed just as in the larger actions. If children find these difficult, there are several first steps which can be tried.

Fine motor skills

Writing

For writing activities, make sure that desks and chairs are

- secure with no wobble
- at the correct height (elbow height for desks, and chairs which allow feet to rest on the floor – no dangling legs to hinder balance).

When the children are writing, you should

- allow the children to experiment with different pencil grips
- check the position of the paper and the desk space for a left-handed child
- fix the paper securely to the desk with Blu-Tack
- try an inclined board for writing or drawing, especially if copying something from the board, because this helps tracking and saves the children losing their place.

Cutting

For cutting activities

- make sure the scissors *will* cut
- have left-handed scissors available
- use firm paper or card
- provide guidelines for cutting if any accuracy is required.

Playing the piano

Lots of activities are good for finger strengthening and dexterity, including playing the piano.

The child should sit securely so that concentration can go to the fingers. Using just one hand at first, the child should play three or four notes slowly up the scale and down, trying to keep the palm of the hand still. Then try with the other hand – then two hands for fun. Simple tunes like 'Jack and Jill' or 'Ding Dong Bell' give lots of pleasure, for success in moving the fingers and hands well gives a musical feedback.

An electric keyboard is not so good because the notes are too light and don't require the same strength in the separate finger actions.

Drawing

Children enjoy drawing letters or pictures and making models in wet sand (Photo 9). Wet sand is better than dry as it gives some resistance and therefore offers strengthening to weak fingers. Making a dam or roadways in the sand is excellent because of the potential for strengthening that this kind of activity holds.

Photo 9 Moulding wet sand

Moulding

Moulding clay interests children who like to make dishes or pots. The rolling action helps strengthen the hands and if there are long strands to be coiled, this helps dexterity and crossing the midline of the body as well as hand dominance. As with the writing activities, it is important to check the height of the benches; also check the malleability of the clay.

Threading

Children can thread either beads or pasta rolls. The beads can be different sizes to arrange into patterns so that sequencing of shapes is helped. Threading is aiming practice on a very small scale. It can be very challenging if the holes are small; however, this activity does help directionality and dexterity. Some children find this kind of work, which requires two hands to work together at the midline of the body, frustratingly difficult and so this can be a useful activity for observation and assessment.

Look for and correct

- children who shut one eye or who tilt their heads to align the string with the bead; the difficulty may stem from a visual impairment rather than a spatial awareness one
- check that the pincer grip is being used, not the whole hand clutching the string; if this is difficult have lots of picking up Lego practices – the firm toy is easier than the floppy thread.

Pincer grip activities

Counting sweets or marbles into a jar is a challenging activity if the jar is held and the lid screwed on and off. This is because it happens at the midline of the body and needs two-handed coordination.

Winding a yo-yo similarly involves the child holding an object with one hand away from the body and using the other hand in a circular motion at the midline. Some children find this very difficult but they will often persevere because it is something they would like to be able to do.

Thus there are lots of activities to help children with movement difficulties. It is important that the activity is worthwhile in the children's eyes, i.e. that it has a purpose and that success can be seen. Regular practice can achieve amazing results but the exercises have to be done properly, with due attention paid to poise and the quality of each movement. Once gross and fine motor skills have been practised separately, they can come together as in the following rhyme which can be used as a daily warm up.

Helping children with movement difficulties

Daily Warm Up

Stand up straight, stretch up high
Wiggle those fingers in the sky,
Wave your arms, put them down,
Clap your hands, and turn around!

Stamp those feet, crouch down low,
Count up to ten and off we go,
One, two, three, four, five, six,
seven, eight, nine and now it's ten.

(spoken)
Hooray!
Now we're ready for the day,
Ready for work and ready for play!

Anne Revels

Daily Warm Up

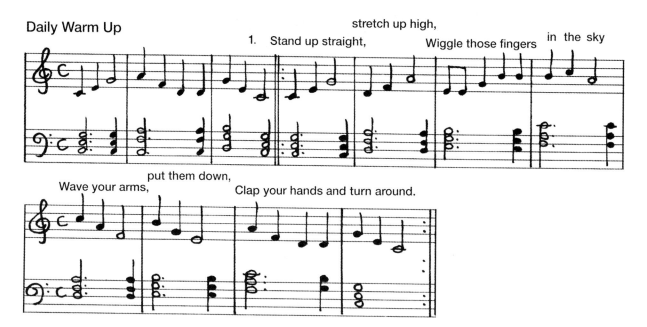

2. Stamp those feet, crouch down low,
   Count up to ten and off we go,
   One, two, three, four, five, six,
   seven, eight, nine and now it's ten.

   (spoken)
3. Hooray!
   Now we're ready for the day,
   Ready for work and ready for play!

Anne Revels's poem makes an ideal movement or perceptual-motor start to each day. It is fun to do, the rhythm intrigues the children, gets the momentum going and gives a lovely sense of working together. It is based on simple movements and if the speed is sensitively gauged, every child should be able to join in. The poem encourages lots of body and kinaesthetic awareness through the children feeling where the body parts are in relation to each other and where they are in the space around them. There are balance challenges in stretching high and crouching low and the stamping helps children with a poorly developed sense of body awareness feel where their feet are. It can be done standing by a desk or table, takes up little room, brings forth a smile and engenders a feeling of everyone beginning the day confidently with a sense of purpose (Photo 10). Perhaps substituting another ending, e.g. 'Now we are finished for today, we've worked well and we're off to play', could mean that the poem could give a positive finish to the day as well.

NB Having a rhythmical activity means that there is momentum and flow to help the children overcome the 'sticky bits'. This is why there are so many rhymes and jingles interspersed throughout this text. They also help children with poor short-term memories to cope. Lots of ideas like this are contained in the lesson plans in Chapter 4.

This kind of daily repetition *provides opportunity for regular physical activity,** and because children appear to settle better after activity, it *supports other areas of learning** (DfEE 2000).

Photo 10 Waving arms

Chapter 2

Developing sensory integration

This chapter will explain how fun activities can be designed to help perception and sensory integration. This is important because children have to perceive cues from the environment accurately through their senses and use these pieces of information together if their movement patterns are to be effective and efficient in different environments. Some children can do a movement quite well if it happens in the same place and if it requires the same spatial interpretation, i.e. if it is grooved or habitual, but are lost when there are new environmental cues. An example of this would be the child who can kick a ball into a goal mouth during practices, and possibly from a standing start, but who becomes flustered and inept when this has to happen in a game, i.e when the environmental cues are shifting and adjustments have to be made.

What kind of information comes through each sense? Figure 6 illustrates the sensory-motor pathway.

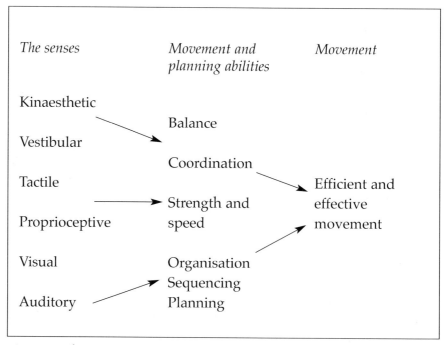

Figure 6 The sensory-motor pathway

While all of these senses work together, it is possible to design activities specifically to help each one. Suggestions for these are given below the description of each sense and the effect each has on movement.

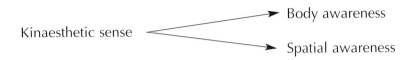

The body awareness part of the kinaesthetic sense relays information about where body parts are in relation to each other, while the spatial awareness part tells where they are functioning in the space around the body and in relation to objects in that space. (The 'instructions to move' come through the proprioceptors, which are nerves in the muscles and joints which convey positional information). If these sub-components are slow to develop, then the children will be clumsy. If children lack body awareness, they will feel and so move their bodies as a whole entity rather than as segmented parts which can move independently of each other. As a result, their actions are awkward and ungainly. If they lack spatial awareness, they will misjudge distances between themselves and objects in space. This means that when they sit down, they clatter into their chair because their proprioceptors have told them it was nearer than it really was, or they misplace items, e.g. in trying to put a cup on a table they place it insecurely – just hitting the edge of the table rather than on it – or miss the table altogether. If the children are constantly scolded for spilling and breaking things and they don't understand why, their self-esteem plummets.

Simon Says

This game involves the teacher or a chosen leader standing out front and giving the instructions, e.g. 'Simon says, Put your hands on your knees'. With the youngest children, it needs to be taken very slowly to ensure that each child understands the instructions and can respond to them rather than copying the child in front. When the instruction is given without the preface, 'Simon says', the children do not move. This encourages enjoyment and concentration apart from developing body awareness.

As the leader calls out different body parts, it is helpful to take a moment to ensure that everyone knows what the less obvious ones are, e.g. elbows, shoulders and ankles. Lots of 'backs of' suggestions are helpful, because awareness of e.g. backs of heels can very often be omitted and they are important when putting on shoes. Many children have no awareness of their backs at all; this can mean that toilet visits are problematic, with the ones who don't wipe successfully sometimes being called smelly – which does their self-esteem no good at all. Awareness of backs becomes very important for safety when forward rolls are introduced, because then they have to be rounded, otherwise the body will jar as it thumps down onto the mat.

Spinning cone

The spinning cone is an excellent piece of apparatus for helping children to feel their backs; the strength needed to make the cone turn must be applied through the back of the shoulders (Photo 11). Furthermore, the children love it. Adult supervision is usually needed to regulate the queue. Some children find getting in and out of the cone difficult, and will need an adult to help by holding the cone steady. Asking the children to stop the cone at the top of a spin and then to make it 'go the other way' can help both their planning and their control.

Photo 11 Spinning cone

Pencil (i.e. longways) rolling on mats

Teachers should emphasise the toes pushing down, legs straight and long bodies; if the children find this difficult, then hands can be held protectively in front of the chest facing out. They can then help push the body over in the roll so that the face is not so near the ground.

Sausage sizzle

As a progression to the pencil rolling activity, the children are rolled up in mats with heads and feet protruding. They then have to unwind the mat. This means they have to push with their shoulders and backs. An adult needs to oversee this activity. When the child is rolled up, the others repeat 'sausage sizzle' till the 'sausage' manages to unroll him- or herself from the mat.

Rhymes and songs

All sorts of rhymes and songs involve identifying the different parts of the body. Here is a body awareness jingle.

A Body Awareness Jingle

> You can tap on your shoulder, tap on your nose,
> Clap your hands together and do you suppose
>
> You can tap on two elbows, tap on two knees?
> Tap so very gently wherever you please!
>
> You can clap hands together, one, two and three.
> Stretch them out as far as you really can see.
>
> You can shake your left hand and now shake your right.
> Shake them both together with all of your might.
>
> Give them a rest now, hide them away.
> Are you ready? Show them?
> Do it, Hooray!
>
> C.M.

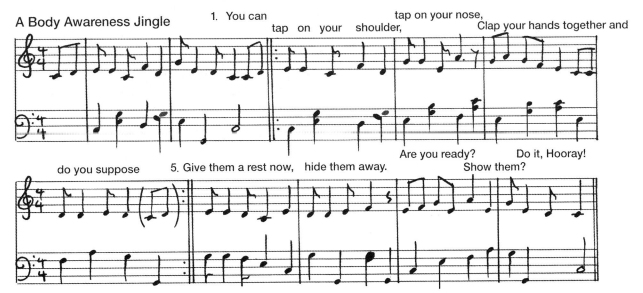

2. You can tap on two elbows, tap on two knees?
   Tap so very gently wherever you please!

3. You can clap hands together, one, two and three.
   Stretch them out as far as you really can see.

4. You can shake your left hand and now shake your right.
   Shake them both together with all of your might.

(The first four verses are sung to the first tune while the last verse has a different tune.)

Activities to help spatial awareness

The purpose of the activities here is to help the child gauge distances accurately and judge the amount of strength, speed and space which is required. These could all be presented as problem-solving activities. What sorts of estimations should the children be able to make?

- Judging the size of step, e.g. how many big or small steps will be needed to reach the other side of the rope river. The children suggest how many they might need and then try.

Photo 12 How many steps will you need to cross the river?

- Judging the length of reaching out, e.g. 'Where will I need to stand to reach the wall?' Again the children take up their estimated position before stretching out to try. This activity helps them judge distances, e.g. in placing a cup on a table, in judging how near to stand to another child in a line.
- Judging the amount of speed, strength and space which is needed to cope with (i.e. avoid, catch, hit, kick) a moving object.

Rolling balls

The children roll a large/small/light/heavy ball to make it stop in a hoop. Gradually increase the distance and reduce the size of the ball so that it travels faster and the children's reactions and movements have to be faster too.

Progressions

First, stand behind a line. Roll a large ball and run round to field it before it crosses a second line (avoid having the children running towards a wall).

Second, stand behind a line and roll a ball to rebound off an upturned bench. Catch it on the rebound – without moving in over the line. If the ball stops inside the line showing that not enough strength has been used, then the children retrieve it and carry it back behind the line to try again.

In these activities the children need to make combined judgements about the speed and strength they need to use to make the ball retrievable. This is also a very good activity to help visual tracking.

Placing quoits over skittles

The children begin by playing hoop-la, i.e. attempting to throw the quoit so that it goes over an upturned pole or a skittle. They stand behind a line and have five or so shots before moving over the line to retrieve any quoits that are on the floor and place them over the skittles. While the hoop-la part is really just for fun, placing the quoits over the skittles gives good practice in judging distances and directions and helps 'letting go', for many children find judging the moment of release very difficult.

A hoop-la stall

In class, the children can make and decorate a hoop-la stall (this could add to the circus theme on p. 65) Children could take it in turns to be in charge of the stall, calling out the jingle to attract custom.

A Hoop-la Jingle

Roll up, Roll up! Come and try,
Throw your hoop to win a prize.
Not too high and not too low,
Try to get it over. You can you know!

Roll up, Roll up! Come and try,
Throw your hoop to win a prize.
Oops, you've missed. It's hard to do.
Try once more and count the rings. What's your score?

C.M.

2. Roll up, Roll up! Come and try,
   Throw your hoop to win a prize.
   Oops, you've missed. It's hard to do.
   Try once more and count the rings. What's your score?

Vestibular sense

The vestibular sense determines the child's ability to balance and is centrally important to skilful movement. Why should this be? Because a good sense of balance is not just useful in activities such as balancing on a bench or riding a bike; balance plays a constant role in sustaining the equilibrium of the body, whether it be in sitting steadily, jumping to catch a ball, even rolling over the ground. This sense tells children where they are in space and how they need to adjust if obstacles appear. Or, if some movement causes them to go off balance, e.g. in slipping on wet grass or going over on an ankle, this sense helps to align the body in the upright position once more. As this sense is so important to all the coping skills required during the day, testing children with simple activities is essential if a difficulty is suspected. If the difficulty persists after practices (and these activities, in terms of what they were, when they were tried and how often they were practised, should be recorded as evidence), then specialist help – perhaps psychologist, optician, physiotherapist or occupational therapist – should be sought. (See also Different ways of recording observations, p. 51.)

Activities to test the vestibular sense

It is a good idea for teachers to try these two activities themselves just to feel the sensations they produce and realise how deceptively taxing they are.

First, ask the children to walk in a straight line, heel–toe, heel–toe, i.e. slowly and carefully placing the heel of the moving foot to the toe of the standing foot. If they have a poor sense of balance, they will sway and have to hold their arms out to prevent themselves toppling over.

Second, the children should stand still and quiet for a moment. Then they raise their arms out to the side and with their eyes closed and in their own time, turn slowly round. They should face the front and hold steady for a moment before opening their eyes.

If any children find these impossible or distressing, teachers shouldn't persevere but get specialist help as soon as possible.

Activities to help the sense of balance

NB Any practice should be done very slowly and carefully with the teacher there ready to support, so that the child feels the correct alignment of the body. Activities should be tried on the floor before using a bench or inclined plank; if heights are introduced, this should be done slowly. It is often more satisfactory to add challenges to benches, e.g. stepping over objects, than to raise the height and cause unease, for this only adds stress and reduces the chance of a movement being done well.

Walking and marching
Any of the walking and marching activities from Chapter 1 will help here.

Swaying
Children stand facing each other, two hands joined. Shift the weight one way so that the body weight balances on one leg, then shift back

to regain the upright position. Sway the other way, then come back to tall standing. Both children go the same way, then opposite ways. Then they can try with one hand joined. Once this is successful, they should increase the lean over so that there is no doubt that they feel an acute change of position.

Progression
Repeat the swaying exercise, but one child turns and has his or her back to the other, thus cutting out visual cues. This needs sensitive cooperation, which may not be suitable for every pair.

Rocking
Linked to this, any rocking activities which are based on losing and regaining balance are helpful. Children enjoy rocking horses, lying on their fronts with hands under shoulders to push up or curled on backs with arms round knees.

Sequence
Each child should build a sequence of three movements and explain then show where the difficult moments in being balanced were. This helps planning and ordering.

Pencil roll
Walk to the edge of the mat, sink down and travel over the mat in a pencil roll, come up to standing well at the end. Keep every action balanced! The transition or adjustment involved in sinking down can cause balance difficulties.

Crawling
Begin by crawling over a mat or a bench, then take up a balanced crawling position. Lift one arm to wave (this keeps the head up) and replace it. (Check that the balanced crawling position has been regained.) Once this has been done with both arms, one hand should lead through the tunnel made by the supporting arm to take the body over into a sideways roll right round till the crawling position is held once more.

Kicking horses
Lean on hands, straighten legs and come back to the crawling position; this is strong work for the arms and hands which should be directly under the shoulders. The more able children can use one leg to swing themselves up into a mini-handstand. This is called Kicking Horses.

Waving legs
Again in the crawling position, wave one leg as a tail, then regain a balanced crawling position. Try the other leg. Bring the waving leg smoothly through to regain a standing position, then run and jump to land on a mat.

These activities are more difficult than they sound, but children who collapse won't be harmed because they are at floor level.

Symmetry

The children will understand those 'keeping balanced' activities if they have been working on symmetry, even in its simplest form. Teachers should ask them to visualise an imaginary line down the centre of their bodies, then try to keep the two sides of their bodies symmetrical, or 'looking exactly the same' as they move. This also pinpoints the midline of their bodies, which is useful for them when they come to activities which have to cross it, e.g. writing, using a knife and fork, tying laces.

But as all activities need balance, any activity done carefully with an awareness of two sides of the body will help. This also helps sequencing and the short-term memory because the children have to retain the instructions for a series of actions.

Transitions

Sometimes discrete movements can be done quite well, but the overall picture lacks any fluency or grace. When that happens it is necessary to look at the transitions or the adjustments which are necessary to join different movements together (Figure 7). If children find they are stumbling, sometimes simplifying the path of the movement helps, i.e. doing it in a straight line rather than changing directions or perhaps having a longer space between actions helps. Sometimes just taking larger or smaller steps is enough to solve the problem.

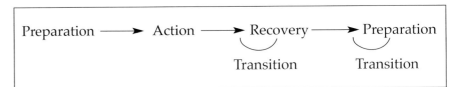

Figure 7 Transitions

Visual sense

The sense of vision is another critically important sense which the children will use to compensate for other difficulties – hence activities which cut out visual cues are used when balance is being tested.

Obviously any sight problems will interfere with deft movement especially in unknown surroundings, but there are less obvious visual difficulties too. These concern functional vision. Some children are easily distracted. They cannot cut out movements in the environment and so find it difficult to concentrate on any one thing. If they spend much of their time seeing what others are doing or looking at leaves blowing on the tree outside, then they lose teaching input and an understanding of what they should be doing next. In this way they lose good examples of organising and planning as well as the content of the lesson. These children are orally bright often with good imaginations but never get any written work completed. In activity sessions, they need a quiet space, facing away from possible distractors, without being isolated from other children. Ideally they should be near the teacher. This applies equally well to lessons in the hall as movement ideas need to be generated there and movement plans require to be made just as ideas and structures are required in story-writing and storytelling.

Mirrors

Often teachers ask whether it helps children if they use mirrors. Certainly they help if the children are checking a body position when they are still, such as, checking if shoulders are level and relaxed when they stand well or to see if their backs are level in the crawling position. However, during movement, the mirror gives an opposite-direction image and can be confusing, especially if the children are unsure of right and left. In my view, it is better to ask the children to spot a point on the wall and use it as a point of reference in actions like turning and coming back to face the front. This strategy also cuts out distractions which occur when other children moving are reflected in the mirror. As even nursery children like to look at how their hair is and how their clothes look, these considerations can supplant the learning that is supposed to be taking place.

Being able to listen is a skill which many children need to develop, especially if the input is coming from behind. In many activities the children need to have this skill as it enables them to make judgements about distance and speed, e.g. how far away something is and how fast it is approaching, for these perceptions may well influence the timing of their responses.

Auditory sense

Activities to help listening to movements that are going on behind

NB As these activities are carried out, teachers should try to prevent the children turning round to see what is happening, because then visual signals may be compensating for poor auditory ones.

All sorts of stalking practices
One child, sitting blindfolded, must listen for any approaching stalker; these can be pirates or lions in the jungle or pirates who are aiming to get hold of the treasure or whatever is being guarded (Figure 8). The littlest ones love stalking to go into the woods for a picnic (snack out-of-doors) when 'The Teddy Bears' Picnic' is played.

'Eyes front' or 'Listen, don't look' game
In this activity the children line up, one behind the other, all facing forward. The child at the front rolls a ball through his or her own legs, then the legs of the children lined up behind. The last one catches the ball, runs round to the front and tunnels the ball again. The activity finishes when the original leader is back at the front. The line should be long enough so that the children at the front have to listen because

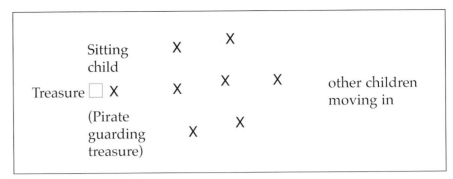

Figure 8 Stalking game

they cannot see what is going on. This is a good mini-game for the end of a lesson. It helps listening, waiting for a turn and remembering what to do when, as well as judging the pace of the oncoming ball.

Noise-sensitive children

Some children listen too hard and become overwhelmed by noises that do not begin to disturb other children. At the cinema, they hear only the rustle of sweet papers or popcorn; in the classroom, even turning pages can make them squirm. In the nursery they will avoid the joinery (hammering) and any other noisy corner.

Activities to help noise-sensitive children
Have the noise-sensitive children play 'soft' percussion, e.g the triangle or the jingles on a tambourine, to accompany a story or movement rhyme. See if they can gradually play the instrument a little louder; if they can, change it for another that can make more sound. As the children are in control of the sound they make, it is hoped that they will learn to tolerate more noise. This could take some time.

Tactile sense The sense of touch using the appropriate amount of strength is poorly developed in some children and this is demonstrated in different ways. First, there are the ones who thump around. They seem to need hard feedback from the environment to tell them where they are in space. These are the children who are constantly sharpening their pencil because they have pressed too hard. They are amazed when things break; when other children won't take hands because they get squeezed, the offending children can't understand why. A second group of children can't bear to be touched. They are touch-sensitive and will wear their socks inside out to avoid the pressure of the seams. Having nails and hair cut is an endurance test which can cause physical pain. A third group can't bear their personal space to be invaded and are understandably upset when other children inadvertently cross their boundary and cause them distress. Sometimes they retaliate by hitting out. All of these tactile difficulties have to be understood and helped.

Activities to help tactile awareness

Children can do lots of experimenting with different textures, e.g. sticking different materials onto a picture to make a collage.

Sand play

Squeezing wet sand to make a shape and breaking it can be contrasted with patting the sand gently to make a model of some kind. Teachers have to explain how the amount of strength affects the outcome. In this way the children see and so come to understand how much strength to use in different situations.

When trailing fingers through dry sand, children can contrast the path made by one finger and by several; again teachers should explain the effect of using too much strength.

Non-threatening contact

Choose activities where the children take hands but keep stretched far away, e.g. Oranges and Lemons. This establishes contact in a non-threatening way. Other useful ideas are for the children to have a common task, e.g. make a parachute billow. In this activity, gradually increasing the number of children so that the space between them is reduced can help those with personal space difficulties, because their attention is held by the parachute rather than being highly conscious of their neighbour's presence.

Deciding how to help children is not easy. It depends on careful observation to see what is amiss. The cause may be in a poorly developed movement ability or it may be due to lack of sensory integration. Careful repeated practice of activities which will help a particular difficulty is the way to proceed.

Proprioceptive sense

The proprioceptors are nerve endings in the muscles which relay information about how far the body parts are from each other and from objects in the space around them. They are fundamental requisites for estimating distances. Children with an acute proprioceptive sense can sit down without looking at the seat because their nerves relay positional information about when to bend and release strength and how to adjust the body in a new position. Without this, children have to turn and look, i.e. to use visual cues and this takes time and explains the hesitancy which observers can note if they are assessing response time. If the children have to rush to keep up with their peer group or to fulfil a second instruction, then their judgements about placing and timing are miscued and consequently their actions are likely to be clumsy.

Activities to help develop the proprioceptive sense

It is important that children have a basic understanding of spatial concepts, including the terms:

- above – below
- over – under
- near – far

- nearer – further
- beside – beyond – behind

All sorts of rhymes including nursery rhymes have 'space words', e.g.

- 'Hey Diddle Diddle' – The cow jumped *over* the moon.
- 'Two Little Dicky-birds' – Peter and Paul fly *behind* the back.
- 'Let's Go Fly a Kite' from *Mary Poppins* – This song is good for expressive language. The kite 'goes up to the highest height' – and the children 'send it soaring to where the air is clear'.

Here are two 'Flying a kite' jingles, to be sung to the tune of 'Daisy Daisy'.

Flying, flying	Flying, flying
Soaring into the sky,	Into the sky so blue
Can you still see it?	Soaring up into the clouds
It's going ever so high	Over and under and through
Hold tightly to the string now	It's a lovely day for flying
Or it will fly away.	So we will keep on trying,
And when you're finished	To make it stay,
Pull it in	Away, away
And wind it up this way.	In the shimmery sky all day.

(The winding in action at the midline of the body needs careful teaching.)

Two other songs which help children appreciate the space 'out there' are 'Somewhere, Over the Rainbow', from *The Wizard of Oz*, and 'I'm Forever Blowing Bubbles'.

Songs like this are always enjoyed. Early Years practitioners usually manage to sing along…this keeps the rhythm going and gives a lovely sense of doing things together.

Chapter 3 will look at ways to record observations and deal with tricky issues such as touching children and giving them a label.

Chapter 3

Teaching and observing movement

The best movement teaching is based on recognising what activities will match then extend the children's abilities and encourage their participation. This involves teachers recognising

- where the children are in terms of their movement/perceptual/ planning abilities and current level of skill
- how the children themselves view their competence and if they understand how they can improve
- how willing the children are to be involved in activity sessions and understanding reasons why this might be a problem.

Teachers have to use their observations and knowledge to know when to give reinforcement activities and when to intervene with fresh challenges.*   (DfEE 2000)

In this respect, teaching children to move and all about movement is the same as any other aspect of teaching. Activities have to be selected with the children's existing and potential level of competence driving the lesson plan, and the detail of individual progress or lack of it has to be assessed and recorded as in any other curriculum area.

Keeping children safe

The important difference in focusing on movement or apparatus is that giving the children challenges, while at the same time keeping them safe, is the central consideration – teachers must plan all the activities and all the apparatus layouts safely. They must be aware that some children will tackle movements that they themselves hadn't thought of and make sure that no matter what, there are enough mats and easy ways down so that children don't get hurt or trapped so that they panic and take risks. All the apparatus has to be secure with no sharp edges or protruding corners or slippery poles. The layout has to ensure that there is room for the children tripping and falling between pieces of apparatus and that approach runs don't mean that children collide. Children's clothing can also cause hazards if loops or hoods catch on apparatus or if laces aren't tied.

From the start, it is important to establish some safety rules.

Specific commands must be obeyed

It is important that the same words are used on each occasion so that the children know what they mean and how they must react, e.g.

Get ready to STOP

means bring the movement to a close. This could mean when individual children have finished their sequence or when everyone has had one turn.

FREEZE means STOP RIGHT THERE!

Establishing the difference between the two commands is a safety mechanism. If, as one example, a child is seen contemplating jumping from apparatus which is too high for his level of competence, or if too many children charge to the same apparatus and bumping looks likely, then the freeze command could prevent an accident. Lots of examples of moving and stopping and moving and freezing should be practised; use only floor activities until the children are sure what each one means. Teachers will also have to consider the intrinsic momentum of movements and be ready with the appropriate command in time, for stopping may be beyond a child's control if a command comes too late.

Beyond this freeze command, however, the children should have as much notice as possible of what they are to do. This is so that they can gather their thoughts and their strength and generally 'get ready to go'. Some children with poor spatial awareness need extra time to check where they are in relation to walls or obstacles. Advance warning allows them to begin to move in a planned and controlled way. It also drives home the message that thinking about how best to move, i.e. planning the most appropriate way, is an important part of moving well.

Have lots of mats

Many children have a good idea of the things they can cope with safely, but others will choose inappropriately. So teachers have to anticipate where there could be danger spots and stay near them. Lots of mats, preferably crash mats, have to be adjacent to climbing frames or under any apparatus which could be dangerous for children with little control or not enough strength to hang on.

Other planning points

- Remember that some children become disorientated by too much rushing around. They lose their spatial cues and become confused. Brief spells of activity interspersed by quiet moments are best for them.
- Sometimes it helps to plan a circuit so that the children can easily see the order of activities to be tackled. Timid children then know that no one will be rushing up behind them or across their path.

- Remember that while some children can't do, there are others who can't plan what it is they wish to do, or organise the resources to let them try. The teacher's role is to know which aspect is problematic and to be ready with appropriate prompts.
- For some children, explaining the logic of the choice of movements can be as helpful as explaining how they should be done, e.g. it is better to do your handstand first, before you run, because balancing is easier when you have been still.
- Check out the school policy on touching children – does this include offering them support on the apparatus or on the floor? (See also Supporting and touching children, p. 58). If so, is there a mechanism for explaining to parents what is involved or the limitations on the programme if this cannot occur?

NB It is vital that teachers cover themselves against any possible accusation, no matter how unlikely this seems.

Using percussion as signals

Using percussion is a good way to develop the children's listening skills: changes in tempo or rhythm or intensity can replace verbal instructions. When there is a quiet activity, e.g. prowling or stalking around, the percussion can be played quietly too. Another advantage of soft playing is that this often calms a class because the children have to listen to hear the sound changes which tell them what to do next. Short spells with lots of contrasting sounds are fun especially when they accompany the children moving freely in space or in and out of obstacles, for then the movement demands are not high and the children are freed to listen and respond in their own way.

All sorts of homemade percussion such as yoghurt pots filled with dried peas or thick elastic bands stretched over plastic ice-cream boxes or large size Toblerone tubes with sliding beans can be used. If the children have made the percussion themselves in the nursery or the classroom, they will have ownership and they will have had the opportunity to listen to the sounds. This may help them appreciate the kinds of movements which the sound suggests. However, real percussion lasts longer and withstands more handling, so it is a good idea to have some. What kind?

- A tambourine (jingles) can signal 'Get ready to...' and the drum skin of either a tambour or tambourine, with either a soft or hard beater, can be used for 'stop'. (Cymbals can be too loud for noise-sensitive children.)
- Indian bells are good for stretching or other slow movements because the sound going on and on encourages continuity.
- Wood blocks are good for jerky movements, e.g. in a puppet dance, for they give a crisp, sharp sound.
- Maracas are good for any continuous action where a definite beat is not required.
- Cymbals rubbed over each other can suggest building up strength and speed; a huge bang, however, may well frighten some of the noise-sensitive children. If it must be used, give warning, e.g. 'Here it comes', so that these children can cover their ears.

Watching and copying

If children are allowed to play the percussion to accompany others as they move, they learn about rhythm and also develop their fine movement skills as they control it (Photo 13). This is very helpful for children with little strength in their hands – they also feel they are in charge. Thus they are having strengthening help unobtrusively and, when they can cope, their self-esteem is boosted. For children who have difficulty planning what it is they wish to do, playing the percussion gives them a moment or two to watch the others moving. Perhaps the teacher could ask one or two children to demonstrate and spell out how their movements are fulfilling the task which has been set? The children are being helped to plan in a subtle way. If the demonstrated movements are within the capability of the percussion children, perhaps everyone could try to copy that sequence. This would increase all the children's repertoires of ideas.

Photo 13 Percussion

Observation schedules

The transitory nature of movement makes observation difficult. Teachers need to know what comprises a good movement pattern and be able to recognise aberrations or aspects of the children's patterns which are different from the norm – always remembering that the normal timing of the acquisition of movement patterns is wide. They also need to know what is causing any difficulty and whether it is likely that it could be eased by maturation. All of these decisions need to be made in the light of the children's age, the amount of experience they have had, and the context which surrounds them. It is really more important to record progress than worry too much about the norm, but tables giving examples of what most children of a particular age can do, do provide a comparative element which can be helpful in ascertaining the severity or range of children's difficulties. An example is in Appendix 1.

The first thing to say is that teachers should try to observe the children in different environments to get a clear picture of their usual coping style. This allows the observer to see whether any other influence could be hampering the children's movements, e.g.

- stress in a new environment
- a new learning activity
- crowding by other children
- noise made by other children
- not understanding what to do
- equipment which could hurt
- not feeling well
- unsuitable footwear, e.g. rigid soles.

There are a myriad of reasons why accurate observation is more taxing than it seems and why assessments might not record a true picture of events.

Observation is important as new learning has to be built on the children's existing competences – even more so if difficulties are suspected. Then the first thing is for teachers to contact the parents, share their concerns and build a plan together; if there is any question of outside specialist help being sought, then all the strictures have to be observed. Providing these other professionals with hard evidence which comes from observation schedules is much more helpful than lots of 'I think this happens when...' indications of difficulty.

Different ways of recording observations

There are different ways of recording and it is always best done unobtrusively so that the children's behaviour is not changed by them knowing they are being watched.

Using sticky labels

If this is the chosen method, teachers and nursery nurses will usually select one or two children to watch carefully; every day as they hear or see something noteworthy, they jot their observations on sticky labels. These recordings are then gathered together and studied so that a picture of the child's usual movement in several environments is gained. At this stage there would probably not be any intervention – this would wait until several days' recordings were made and the results compared – but teachers would be noting the kinds of activities the children preferred to do and those that were avoided. They would also note any circumstance which could alter a child's participation, e.g. having a cold or falling out with a friend and thus avoiding activities where the friend was. Once all of these points had been considered, intervention could take the form of arranging activities so that the children had the opportunity to practise the movements they found difficult or had avoided.

Pulling such observations together allows objective statements to be made. These can be made confidently because there is evidence to show where they came from (Figure 9).

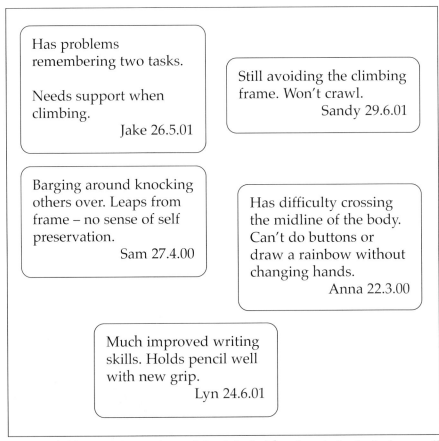

Figure 9 Observation using sticky labels (the date is included as well as the name to help assess progress over time)

Planning the layout of large apparatus to aid observation

The plan shown in Figure 10 has been constructed so that there are opportunities for teachers to observe the children demonstrate their competence in all the basic movement patterns. Care has been taken to space the apparatus to allow falls and so that approach runs do not cross. There are different levels of challenges, e.g. balancing on the broad side of the bench or the narrow side, so there should be some activity which will appeal to each of the children. It can be very helpful for observation purposes to suggest to the children that there is a circuit, for this allows teachers to move with the children and not lose them in the hurly burly of activity. Some rules can help too, e.g. that only four children go on the climbing frame at once. This prevents jostling and pushing which could be dangerous and certainly discourage the more timid children from having a go.

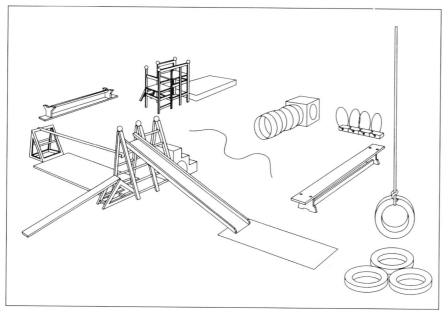

Figure 10 Large apparatus layout

Alongside each piece of apparatus, a list of key observation points which need only to be ticked can make recording quicker (Photo 14). These can be amended for different children.

Photo 14 Observation

A sample page from a record book

Name of child   Date

Apparatus	Yes	No	Comment
• enough strength in pushing up (several tries to get up?)	....	....	....
• balance difficulty (swaying?)	....	....	....
• stride pattern (even and fluent?)	....	....	....
• extra arm movements (curling? holding out in front?)	....	....	....
• tension in the shoulders?	....	....	....

Tunnel			
• unwilling to go into tunnel?	....	....	....
• arms and legs used in a competent crawling action?	....	....	....
• arms unable to pull child out of tunnel?	....	....	....
• legs just dragging behind?	....	....	....
• a pulling action rather than crawling?	....	....	....

Tyres			
• able to run through the spaces?	....	....	....
• using the tyres as balance challenges?	....	....	....
• not coping with the uneven length of strides?	....	....	....
• lacking leg strength?	....	....	....
• avoiding the activity altogether?	....	....	....

Climbing Frame			
• able to climb on using arms to pull up?	....	....	....
• jumps down confidently?	....	....	....
• controls weight in landing?	....	....	....
• fearful of jumping – slithers down?	....	....	....
• no sense of danger – leaps into space?	....	....	....
• avoids the frame altogether?	....	....	....

Swinging tyre			
• gets on easily, copes with the swing?	....	....	....
• holds securely, close to the rope?	....	....	....
• shoulders very tense – can't wait to get off?	....	....	....
• using a great deal of speed and copes?	....	....	....

Time sampling

Name   Tom   Date 1.6.01 Observation focus: Using Pencil
        Activity   Grip

9.10 Painting - large brush in L.H Difficulty in getting brush in pot.
9.15 Wandering around asks if its snack time - encourage to make snack.
9.20 Can't spread butter on bread - lacks strength - abandons job.
9.25 At water, no pouring, just skiddles.
9.30 Can't settle at storytime, restless, doesn't listen
9.35 Wanders off to look out of window.

Figure 11 Time sampling

In this method, what the child is doing every 2 or 5 minutes over 30 minutes or so is recorded. The observer notes what the child chooses to do rather than trying to assess the quality of what is being attempted (Figure 11). From the completed schedule, information about things the child avoids could pinpoint areas of concern, e.g. the child who never attempted climbing could lack leg strength. The schedule can be planned to look at social interactions or incidents such as hitting out or falling over, i.e. any aspect can be the focus of this kind of observation. It provides a tally or level of incidence of something happening, and shows where an assessment looking at the quality of performance could usefully be focused.

Video-recording

Perhaps the most satisfactory evidence comes from video-recording the children, because the pause and replay facilities can counteract the transitory nature of movement which makes observation so difficult. Even if the children are aware they are being filmed and as a result produce movements of a higher standard than usual, that's great, for it shows what they *can* do. If this is markedly different from their usual performance, it clues the observer to the fact that some other cause is influencing their competence.

The film allows more than one person to observe and so there is material for discussion. This gives the new observer confidence, especially if worries are to be shared with parents. Video is also excellent for recording the children's competence before and after an intervention programme because this shows the children and possibly their parents how they have improved.

NB It is essential to have the parents' permission, preferably in writing, before video-recording their children. It is also best if the children don't know in advance that they are to be filmed. One child who did find out borrowed her older sister's new shoes and as they were several sizes too big, she couldn't move well at all. Her mother was furious with the child and with the nursery staff for not noticing before the video was made. She refused permission for the video to be shown beyond the nursery class. Everyone was upset and much of the pleasure was spoiled.

Observation, assessment and intervention

Having made observations using different schedules and/or various modes of gathering evidence, the next stage is to analyse these to identify the difficulties and then to choose exercises, activities and lessons which will give specific help. (Suggestions for these are in Chapters 1 and 4.)

If the required help is minimal, it can probably be given unobtrusively over time as part of usual daily inputs. The children may not even realise they are having special help. But if the children's difficulties are causing real concern, then the parents' permission and cooperation is best sought at an early stage so that a shared programme of activities can be selected and practised. Teachers may need to take time to explain

- the child's difficulties
- their specific and wider implications
- details of any special programme
- the importance of regular practice (four sessions of ten minutes daily as a minimum)
- the importance of movements being done correctly
- the kind of support which will be necessary, and
- possibly the length of time likely to be needed to show sustained improvement.

Parental responses

Parents can respond very differently. Listen to just two:

'I knew when Amy was 3 that there was something wrong, but was told I was an overanxious mother. At Primary, the teachers were supportive; they did what they could but there was still no specialist help. Going to Secondary at 12 held lots of horrors – she just couldn't cope with finding classrooms and making new friends. Even after all this time, we still have no specific diagnosis or help...If children behave badly, then help can be found, but if the children are good, then they have to struggle on. It's really most unfair.'

'I wondered why my Jake was to have extra movement lessons. They said he was clumsy – but boys are, aren't they? Anyway, he's just like his Dad and he's managed OK, so what's the fuss?'

Most parents, however, are glad to hear that their children's difficulties have been spotted and that they are to be offered help in school. Indeed they may have been seeking help in the shape of physiotherapy or occupational therapy for some considerable time and may still be in a lengthy queue, for waiting lists can be for years. Other parents will resent any implication that their child has a movement learning difficulty and consider any intervention unnecessary and intrusive. Some teachers, suspecting this response, have tempered their approach by saying, 'We would like to offer your child a place on a special programme...' and not mention difficulties till the effects of the programme have been evaluated. It is hoped that by this time they may be reduced. This strategy avoids confrontation and may invoke cooperation. After all, teachers don't have to ask if they wish to give extra help in maths or language. While teachers would advocate total openness at all times, they would not want to deny giving appropriate help to any child. If there is likely to be a problem, then the head teacher must be involved so that the best way forward is found.

Activities at home

There is no doubt that if parents *are* willing to practise exercises regularly and carefully at home, then improvement in the child's performance can happen faster. However, there are several dangers which are best aired.

First, parents may overdo the practice time. Then everyone becomes tired, cross and even resentful.

Second, there are so many other things to do at home that the exercises are missed out or done irregularly. Many parents are unwilling to admit this has happened because they feel they have let their child down and so teachers get a false sense of what is going on. They suspect that the exercises are not working effectively when, in fact, they haven't been done at all.

Third, the exercises are seen as a punishment for 'not getting it right' and practice time is extended and no longer fun. Sometimes children are not allowed out to play till they are finished and this is self-defeating because the quality of the practice deteriorates and the outdoor play activity could be beneficial too.

NB The length of time, the regularity *and* the stress-free nature of any practice time has to be established, otherwise the programme is best kept to school time.

Giving children a label

Most people are unwilling to give an Early Years child a label because of the uncertainty of how maturation, intervention and practice will interact to improve the child's competence in moving well. There is also the vexed realisation that a diagnostician might apply a label fitting some but not all of the aspects, or even fit the diagnosis to his/her understanding of a condition. The diagnosis of movement difficulties would be likely to be dyspraxia (see Appendix 2), yet not all paediatricians or family doctors agree on what this is. Some will give the diagnosis to any child with movement learning difficulties, while others insist on seeing the discrepancy between the child's score on intellectual and performance IQs, one of the key signs of dyspraxia.

Yet the condition is generally understood in most schools now and information is readily available (see Bibliography). This means that a label alerts teachers to the different aspects of the child's difficulties and these in turn allow useful classroom strategies and interaction skills to be selected (Macintyre 2000, 2001a, 2001b). Parents too must be confident that the correct steps will be taken. If a specific diagnosis is given (and some parents are just so relieved because they have feared something much worse), then they can get together with others who have children similarly labelled; this prevents isolation and gives some comfort through recognising that their child is not alone, in fact that 8–10 per cent of children have some degree of dyspraxia. The best news is that these children can be helped and certainly early intervention programmes are the way to make this happen.

Supporting and touching children

One of the central aims for children with poor body and spatial awareness is that they feel and (it is hoped) internalise the correct alignment of the body as it moves in space. This is essential if they are to be able to move in a balanced, controlled and coordinated way (Photo 15). In this era of not touching children, this kind of support may be problematic. If parents can watch a movement session and be

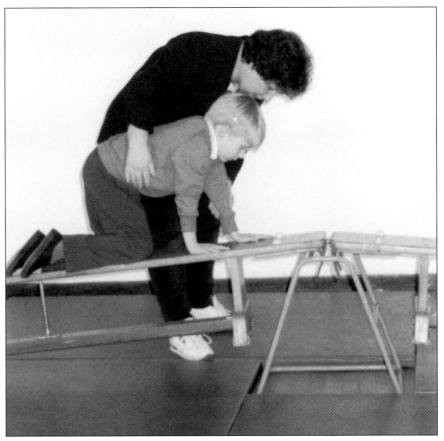

Photo 15 Supporting to help the child feel balanced

58

reassured that 'support' probably means a gentle alteration of the position of a limb, or a hand taken when the child attempts something for the first time, then their written permission can be gained – but this still has to be checked out with the head teacher and considered alongside school policies. If physical support is not possible, then programmes to help are likely to take longer to be effective. This is unfortunate as the benefits of being able to move well are

- good posture and through that better health
- social confidence stemming from being able to join in
- greater confidence across the curriculum
- increased ability to carry out everyday living skills at home
- most important of all, raised self-esteem.

Ideas for lesson plans which aim to achieve all of these things follow in Chapter 4.

Chapter 4

Lots of lesson plans

Ideally, the children should have a daily lesson of about 15–20 minutes. If only a small group from the class are taking part, perhaps the programme could happen when the class administration is being done so that they don't miss out on other teaching. Depending on the arrangement, i.e. the length and regularity of lessons, the kinds of difficulties which most of the group display, and the possibility of getting the hall and suitable apparatus, the following lessons can be taken one at a time as they stand, or selections from a variety of lessons can come together, thus providing contrasting kinds of movement experiences.

It is vitally important that the children have the opportunity to be involved in different kinds of activities so that a full range of competences can be developed. In expressive movement the children learn to appreciate movement, very often through associated language, and to move in ways which develop their imaginations. In this mode there is no apparatus to cope with and so coordination can develop with no extraneous demands. Then there are the more gymnastic type of movements where the basic movement patterns are carried out on large apparatus. These provide balance and timing challenges and help confidence as well as competence. Lastly there are the mini-games skills which will let the children handle small apparatus such as bats and balls and so they learn to cope with moving equipment which presents its own set of demands.

Teachers may allow a variety of experiences to happen within each lesson or different kinds of lessons can be blocked. This is usually easier to organise. The important thing is to provide a balanced programme over time, and to provide learning experiences which will allow children to fulfil the criteria set out in curricular documentation. These emphasise the children doing with understanding (*5–14 Guidelines*)* and the lessons here provide opportunities for discussion and for links to classroom themes and practices so that transfer of learning may occur. There is also plenty of opportunity for children of different abilities to learn together.*

Young children love rhymes and jingles for expressive movement and the first group of lessons are based around these. Each part should be taken slowly and can be repeated to give the children time to feel the movements. Alternatively percussion can be played between each line. The children would probably find it helpful to learn the jingle first with lots of emphasis on the quality of the words which is then transferred to the quality of the movement. Pictures can help to extend understanding, e.g. the children may never have seen a firefly or a wren in the 'Look in the Garden' jingle.

NB Criteria based on the DfEE (2000) publication, *Curricular Guidance for the Foundation Stage* and the *Curriculum and Assessment Guidelines: Expressive Arts 5–14* published by the Scottish Office (SOEID 1992) are shown in each lesson as general learning outcomes and are followed by specific learning outcomes which can form assessment criteria for each lesson.

Lesson plan 1

Look in the Garden

Let's look in the garden. What do we see?
A lovely, floaty butterfly, a zooming, buzzy bee.

A caterpillar crawling, ever so slow
And over there a firefly with wings all aglow.

On the grass two blackbirds, squabbling again,
And underneath the flowers is a tiny jenny wren.

A squirrel in the tall tree climbing up high.
Can you see his bushy tail and sparkling little eye?

Close your eyes and tell me, what did you see?
Remember three small creatures. Can you tell them now to me?

C.M.

Look in the Garden

1. Let's look in the garden. What do we see? A

lovely, floaty   butterfly, a   zooming, buzzy   bee.

2. A caterpillar crawling, ever so slow
   And over there a firefly with wings all aglow.

3. On the grass two blackbirds, squabbling again,
   And underneath the flowers is a tiny jenny wren.

4. A squirrel in the tall tree climbing up high.
   Can you see his bushy tail and sparkling little eye?

5. Close your eyes and tell me, what did you see?
   Remember three small creatures. Can you tell
   them now to me?

General learning outcomes

- The children's appreciation of the natural environment should be extended.*
- The children should be involved in observing, reflecting, describing and responding.*

Specific learning outcomes and assessment points

The children should be able to

- show different qualities of hand movements
- recall three creatures and tell their names
- show the kinds of movements their chosen creatures would make.

Organisation

Children sitting comfortably, hands held in front. (Allow those with poor stability to lean against the wall or sit on a beanbag if it offers good support.) Teacher in front demonstrating movements as the jingle is said.

NB Children should watch their hands all the time except in the memory part at the end.

Butterfly
Hands facing the floor, cross thumbs over each other. Hands move up, down and sideways as wings – emphasise light movements interspersed with stillness to suggest floating.

Buzzy bee
Fingers curled – index fingers pointing – show contrasting darting actions. Take time to emphasise where darting can go – use space words such as above, beyond, behind and below to help spatial awareness and directionality. Children can rise onto their knees or move over the room to let the zoom have more effect.

Caterpillar
Hands placed flat on floor – hands move in caterpillar action, i.e. heel of hand moving towards fingers, then fingers stretch out again.

NB If this is too difficult substitute, 'A slimy snail is crawling' in the jingle and have the children put one hand on top of the other (shell) and move the hands forward together on the floor.

Firefly
Hold one hand behind the other to suggest length and thinness (contrast to width of butterfly) and fingers move lightly again (flicker) to suggest flight and lightness in hovering.

Blackbirds
The two hands are held slightly apart and the fingers 'squabble'. Once the children have the idea of the rapid movement of the fingers they can try it with a partner, to mimic two blackbirds squabbling.

Jenny wren
The hands curl together very small except for the pinkies (fourth fingers), which make the short, standing-up tail.

Squirrel
The children stretch one arm up to make a tree and make the other fingers climb up – quickly and lightly.

Memory check
Children curl up small, eyes closed, and say aloud the three creatures that they liked best. This is a short-term memory check and a useful way to assess retention of ideas.

Movement
Once the children can do this while sitting, larger butterfly or buzzy bee movements can take them all over the room – but the emphasis on the quality of the movement should not be lost.

Linked classroom and home activities

The children could gather pictures from magazines to make a wildlife collage.

At home they could ask 'Who has seen…this year?' and tally the results.

Story (moral) 'The Eagle and the Wren'
The story is that the eagle boasts that since he is the most powerful bird, he will be able to fly higher than any other. Unknown to him, however, the wren hides on his back and when the eagle is exhausted, the wren takes off and flies even higher. Lots to discuss!

The Clown

Lesson plan 2

I'm in the circus, jolly and bright
My trousers are baggy,
I look such a fright.
Hooray, Hooray, Hooray, Ha.

I juggle three balls, all in the air.
I'm smiling and happy,
With bright orange hair.
Hooray, Hooray, Hooray, Ha.

Come to my circus, and dance round the ring,
Climb in the trapeze,
Where acrobats swing.
Hooray, Hooray, Hooray, Ha.

Gallop like horses, grab on the rein,
It's great fun this circus,
We'll come back again.
Hooray, Hooray, Hooray, Ha.

C.M.

2. I juggle three balls, all in the air.
    I'm smiling and happy,
    With bright orange hair.
    Hooray, Hooray, Hooray, Ha.

3. Come to my circus, and dance round the ring,
    Climb in the trapeze,
    Where acrobats swing.
    Hooray, Hooray, Hooray, Ha.

4. Gallop like horses, grab on the rein,
    It's great fun this circus,
    We'll come back again.
    Hooray, Hooray, Hooray, Ha.

General learning outcomes

- The children should take on different roles so that they develop empathy with others.*
- The children should re-enact a story with props.*

Specific learning outcomes and assessment points

The children should be able to

- role-play their parts in the circus
- gallop (precursor to learning to skip) alone and with a partner.

Organisation

Verse 1

Children move around with large steps as if they had baggy trousers and large feet. (Use a tambour to help the rhythm of pacing out the large steps.) Note those who overbalance and see if they find coming back to standing well difficult.

Verse 2

The children imitate the juggling movement or they can try it, preferably using airflow balls – just for fun. They then point to their hair and ruffle it. They should also rub the backs of their heads to help body awareness of that less usual part.

Verse 3

The teacher or one child as ringmaster beckons the children into the circus tent. They form a ring and gallop round – like circus horses. They then point up to where the trapezes are and make their arms swing or do a roll or attempt a cartwheel or some other action to represent acrobats.

Verse 4

Horses galloping once more – this time in twos. One is the horse (ropes laid over the shoulders from back to front, then under the arms to form the reins) while the other child leads the horse by the reins round the circus ring. Change over for the next try.

NB Notice children who fall over or who can't use different feet to lead the stepping action in verse 1. They are likely to have balance or side dominance difficulties which need to be helped. Also in the tandem activity at the end, note whether the children can retain the space between the horse and the rider with the reins. If not, this can be tried with large plastic hoops as they stay stiff and regulate the distance, but ropes which can be used to urge the horse on are more realistic and more fun.

Linked classroom activities

In class the children can make trapezes from straws and sticky paper and cut out figures to sit on the crossbar. The teacher or older children can make a Big Top for the little ones to decorate or suspend the trapezes from a string across the room. Stories about the circus and discussions, asking e.g. 'How would you like to live in a circus?' or 'Are clowns always happy, do you think?' or 'What happens if they feel sad on a performance night?' all help the understanding of a very different way of life and stimulate a great deal of interest. The children could also make life-size draw arounds and dress them as clowns. This helps planning and ordering getting dressed, which some children find difficult.

Lesson plan 3

The Puppet

I'm a small wooden puppet
All tied up with string
I lie in my box only able to sing!

It's so sad I can't dance,
For I'd love to be free,
But elbows and knees are tied up you see.

Now I'm pulling that string
And I'll toss it away,
And now I shall dance all the hours of the day!

But what is that noise
That sound that I hear?
It's calling me back to my wee box I fear!

So I crumple right down
And tuck elbows in tight,
And have a wee sleep, shut my eyes, say 'Goodnight'.

C.M.

This lesson focuses on body awareness and gross motor skills, particularly moving jerkily with awareness of elbows, knees and wrists, so before the lesson, it helps to discuss what a wooden puppet looks like and how it moves. Teachers could show a real one or have a colourful picture. Stories such as Pinocchio make a useful link, but this lesson really needs to think about the puppet and the puppeteer if the extension part is to be used.

General learning outcomes

- The children should learn the language of movement* as they do the actions, e.g. pulling, tossing, crumpling and jerking.
- The children should understand different emotional responses,* e.g. sadness, freedom, resignation.

Specific learning outcomes and assessment points

The children should be able to

- move like a puppet with stiff arms and legs and then show a contrasting, free type of movement when the strings are tossed away
- show their body awareness of elbows and knees, by being able to identify them and by being able to move jerkily and rhythmically, using arms and legs fully in flexion and extension
- listen hard so that they change actions in time with the words.

Organisation

Verses 1 and 2

Children lie on floor inside their box – all floppy. They rub their elbows and knees as these parts are mentioned in the jingle.

Verse 3

The children rise up and step out of their box, lifting their knees high, pull the strings from their elbows and knees, roll them up and toss them away. (The children may find the rolling action difficult – it's a very useful one to practise as it happens at the midline of the body.) The children should dance all over the room (jingles on a tambourine as accompaniment or a tape of lively music?) when they become free, but all the time they are listening for the 'sound' that tells them to go back to their original space.

Verses 4 and 5

On the sound (cymbals rumbling – not too loud because of noise-sensitive children), the children go back to their original space, i.e. their box, rub their elbows and knees and find that their strings have appeared again, then they 'crumple' down, and shut their eyes.

Progression and development

The children work in twos, one as a puppet, the other as the puppeteer. As a general learning outcome, the children should learn to negotiate and cooperate.

For specific learning outcomes, the children should be able to move, be aware of how their partner moves and adapt to the space and the speed of that other person. The children should also be able to move jerkily to counts of eight beats with balance and control.

The puppet is in the box and rises to eight counts 1 and 2 and 3 etc. Only move on the count, unfolding and rising jerkily. The puppeteer (possibly an older child?) has to control the strings as he or she counts.

As the puppet unties the strings, the puppeteer has to let go and run to hide while the puppet does a free dance.

The puppeteer then makes the sound recalling the puppet to the box and the pair move together again, the puppeteer flopping over the exhausted puppet to finish.

Linked classroom activities

In class the children can make finger puppets (the finger has to move jerkily to make it work), and use these to have conversations or to tell stories (oral storytelling).

Lesson plan 4

Circles

Run into a circle,
Join hands wide.
Then dash into the centre,
Let no one get inside.

Turn around three times,
Then stay at rest,
Try not to wiggle,
That would be best!

Run to the outside,
Have you found your spot?
Stamp your feet now
Do it quite a lot.

Can you reach your friend
And make a lovely ring?
If you can do that
It's time to sit and sing!

C.M.

General learning outcomes

- The children should appreciate shapes and how shapes stay the same despite changing size.*
- The children should show awareness of themselves and others,* i.e. move in line with others who are by their sides.

Specific learning outcomes and assessment points

The children should be able to

- understand the concept of circles changing size but retaining a shape (developing spatial awareness)
- retain their balance after turning (with eyes open and eyes closed).

Organisation

Lines 1 and 2
Children run from the edge of the room to join hands in a large circle. Check the shape. Ask the children to drop their hands and rejoin them several times, the challenge being to see if they can retain the shape of the circle. This is good for the development of laterality or awareness of what is happening at the side.

Lines 3 and 4
Keeping hands joined, the children move quickly into the centre. Now they have their arms by their sides, but keep a tight circle shape.

Verse 2

Keeping narrow, they individually turn round three and a half times, finishing facing out. They should hold that balance till they are steady (eyes open or closed).

Verse 3

They run back to their original place and stamp their feet. They enjoy this and it helps those who need strong feedback from the environment to help their spatial orientation.

Verse 4

The children reform their circle. Ask if it is the same size and shape and see if the children can adjust it! Once more this involves them in awareness of things happening at the side.

Linked classroom activities

In fairly large groups of eight or so, the children hold hands and try to make different shapes such as a triangle, square and rectangle as well as different sizes of circles. This can be great fun if the teacher calls out the shape and the children have to form it without letting go hands.

Lesson plan 5

Winter Time

Today it is freezing,
Just look at my nose!
It's all red and shiny
And everyone knows
It's Jack Frost that's been out
And made us feel chill,
But we'll rub it and rub it,
He won't make *us* ill.

Our fingers are tingling
Our toes are too,
Everything's hurting,
What shall we do?

We'll shake our arms and legs about,
One, two, three!
Is that any better? No?
Then come and dance with me!

Round and round and round we skip
This way and that,
Pulling on gloves
And our woolly hats.

We will keep on skipping
Till we are all aglow,
And we'll tell Jack Frost
To GO! GO! GO!

C.M.

General learning outcomes

- The children should appreciate where their body parts are in relation to each other.*
- The children should understand the timing and planning of movements.*
- The children should be aware of the sequence of events to help planning and organising skills.*

Specific learning outcomes and assessment points

The children should be able to

- skip in twos, either with inside hands joined, both facing forwards, or for the most able children, facing each other and skipping round in a circle
- follow the rhythm accurately as the actions in the first part are not difficult.

Organisation

Verse 1

The children point to their noses – accurately – and rub gently with the palms of their hands as they say the rhyme.

Verse 2

The children hold out one arm and the opposite leg then change over.

Verse 3

On the spot they shake out arms and legs trying to maintain balance as they do.

Verses 4 and 5

Free skipping – acting out pulling on hats and gloves. Skip quickly then come to a halt to point, and shout out, 'GO, GO, GO!'

Linked classroom activities

In class the children can discuss the properties of clothes for wintry days, e.g. what makes 'wellies' waterproof? Where does wool for warm hats and gloves come from?

The children can draw icicles and flakes of snow to make a winter collage. Another activity could be making birdcakes and feeding the birds.

Lesson plan 6

Fireworks

Come and join our fireworks party,
It's on Friday, that's quite soon.
We'll have it at night,
So don't get a fright
When rockets whizz and zoom.

We'll dance around the bonfire
And watch the sparks go high
And the smoke will swirl
And the Catherine wheels twirl,
As we dance around the Guy.

We'll say 'ooh' as we hear the bangers
And 'weee' as the rockets fly,
And the moon will stare down
With a grumpy frown
From a glittering, shining sky.

It will be a magic party,
You will be glad you came,
It only happens once a year
Isn't that a shame?

For it's lovely in the evening
All together having fun,
It's the very best way to romp and play
When summer days are done!

C.M.

General learning outcomes

- The children should learn to move with imagination, coordination and control.*
- The children should use physical activity to support other areas of learning (safety).*

Specific learning outcomes and assessment points

The children should be able to

- show the contrasting qualities of the different fireworks
- demonstrate the swirling smoke and the happiness of the children dancing round the Guy.

Organisation

The setting is shown in Figure 12.

The children decide which kind of firework they would like to be and go into one of four groups as shown in Figure 12. Each group performs in turn.

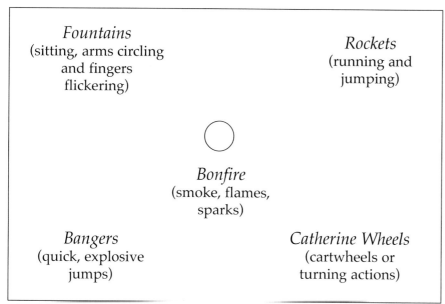

Figure 12 Firework night

Rockets
Strong jumping is needed for zooming and whooshing, with the children meeting the floor safely and curling up to represent dying out.

Catherine wheels
Turning actions are required, e.g. standing with arms held wide and turning with increasing then decreasing speed while maintaining balance. Some children might attempt cartwheel-type actions but this would be too difficult for most.

Fountains
In a group shape, children use their arms in a circling action, i.e. rising and spreading then falling. Fingers 'flicker' to portray the sparks.

Bangers
Explosions are created by either jumping or punching the air with clenched fists to obtain a sudden strong action. Some children can sit to make a group shape. This helps group awareness.

Bonfire
The children love to make the firework sounds as they move in turn to show what each does. After their turn, they all move in to circle the bonfire. One child comes in to light the fire with a long torch (pretend or use a skittle or make one in the classroom). Some children could make the jagged shapes of the twigs and branches of the bonfire while others practise the swirling, rising and billowing movements of the smoke. As the fire takes hold, all the children become flames, rising and sinking to show the movement of the flames.

The fire then gets out of control and sparks shoot off in different directions. Some children then fetch imaginary buckets of water and put the fire out just in time – or the fire engine can be called – with accompanying sounds.

Linked classroom activities

Classroom discussions could involve the fun and danger of fireworks and bonfires, and people who help us such as firefighters. This can lead to more general discussions about safety in the home.

Links could be made with the ambulance or hospital corner in the nursery.

Here are two rhymes for *you* to use as a basis for making lesson plans.   *Lessons 7 and 8*

Summertime

We are so glad it's summer,
For we get out to play,
We love to run and skip and jump
All the hours of the day.

Sometimes we go to the park to play
On the swings or on the slide,
We climb the trees as high as we please
It's great to be outside!

Sometimes we go to the seaside
And build castles on the sand,
Then we dig a moat and make seaweed float;
Life is certainly grand!

Sometimes we go to Granny's,
And then we get a big kiss
She gives us sweets and lots of treats
We wish every day was like this.

But when summer days are over
And autumn says, 'I'm here'
Then we'll think of bonfires and fireworks too,
And welcome it in with a cheer!

C.M.

Counting to Ten

Let's count out some numbers
One, two and three.
Do we know any more?
Let's try and see!

The very next numbers are four, five and six
Start at number one again and count up – let's be quick!

One, two, three, four, five, six.

What a lot of numbers! Are there any more?

There's seven and eight and nine and ten.

Hide all those fingers . . . then we'll count them again.

Lessons using small games apparatus

Children of all ages enjoy working with their own choice of small apparatus and it is a good idea to begin every lesson with a short spell of free practice when they do just that. To avoid crowding – racing to one spot to get the large balls is a usual gambit! – an assortment of apparatus can be shared among hoops spread round the periphery of the hall.

What kind of apparatus is suitable?

- balls of all kinds and sizes – foam, rubber, airflow, tennis and volleyballs, but not basketballs as they can hurt those who get in the way!
- bats – small and large, wooden and cork because they are light, yet make a satisfying sound which helps the rhythm of each shot
- shuttlecocks – they don't run away
- skipping ropes – short and long in case the children want to make a group game; one or two with beanbags tied to the end can make a spinning and jumping game
- hoops for bowling or climbing through
- beanbags for throwing, catching and sliding along the floor
- quoits for tossing or bowling or playing hoop-la
- waste paper baskets for aiming practices.

Lesson format

Lessons could follow the format of

- free choice with a variety of small apparatus
- skill practice which has specific teaching points
- a mini-game.

Some general points

Free choice

As the initial part of the lesson is free choice, only general teaching points can apply to all the children, e.g. 'Keep your apparatus near you', thus emphasising control rather than skill, or 'Sometimes move quickly and sometimes slowly', to let the children see the effect that different speeds have on the particular apparatus they have. Sometimes the children can demonstrate their activity to the others, if, for example, they have thought up an unusual way of moving their apparatus around the hall in a controlled way. The free practice should be done in brief spells with an apparatus changeover which needs to be organised, e.g. 'Stand beside a partner who has a different piece of apparatus. Change over.' This is quicker than having the children put their apparatus back in the hoops and selecting another piece, for this can mean time spent deliberating, even arguing, about the next choice.

Skill practice

Once a couple of free practice changeovers have been made, then the children need to be helped to learn a specific skill such as throwing and catching a ball or bowling a hoop to a partner or aiming airflow balls into a basket. The selection will depend on the needs of the particular group of children.

At the end of the lesson some kind of mini-game is always popular – the type can link to the main skill practice or be a contrasting game.

NB Avoid letting the children choose the teams, otherwise the same children will be left out. It's a good idea to distribute coloured bands as the children enter the hall. This means that the teams are already chosen – because the handout has been carefully planned by the teacher in advance so that each colour has the same number of more and less able players.

Sometimes the children enjoy trying to make their own game. The teacher has usually to give them a designated space and explain that they must have rules for starting the game and restarting it after the ball has gone out of bounds. They also need to decide how a goal or a point will be scored.

Practising balls skills

The main ball skills for very young children are rolling and retrieving, aiming, bouncing and catching, and throwing and catching.

Rolling and retrieving

- Roll a ball ahead and catch it before it crosses a line on the floor. This involves making decisions about how fast to roll the ball, when to retrieve it, where to place the hands to catch the ball, when to turn into the retrieving position and how to stoop and regain a balanced position. These elements can be turned into questions, so making the activity a problem-solving one. The distance between the child and the line and the type of ball used can be varied to increase the challenge. It helps planning if the children have to explain what they are aiming to do.

  NB Some children find releasing the ball difficult, a skill which underlies the throwing action too.
- Stand behind a line. Roll a ball against the face of a tilted bench and retrieve it without crossing the line. This requires judging the amount of speed and strength so that the ball rebounds adequately. This is a good practice for tracking the ball and moving to anticipate the direction of the rebound.
- Children sit in twos, legs astride, facing one another but some distance apart. They roll the ball into the tunnels made by the legs. Emphasise the direction and speed of the roll.
- Similarly, children sit in a circle, legs astride, and choose where to roll the ball. Varying the speed is fun and having two balls going at the same time makes a good mini-game – although the quality of the action is likely to disappear. As a progression, the children can trap the ball by snapping their legs shut.

Aiming
The following activities help visual tracking.

- Skittle alley. This is a progression on the rolling practices as there is an increased distance to the target and a greater need for accurate direction. Some children find balance difficult if the moment of releasing the ball comes too late and the arm winds round the body.

This can be developed into a group game if some of the children put the skittles back in place, some keep the score and others field any balls which have missed the frame altogether. Children love cooperating in this game, especially if they have made the skittles (cardboard tubes filled with pebbles) and the scoring sheets in class. Several lanes can be set up as in a bowling alley and this saves the children running across each other's path to retrieve balls. This is a good maths task too.

- Aiming high. If wicker waste-paper baskets can be tied onto netball stands or wall bars they make splendid baskets for mini basketball-type games. The children then practise bouncing while running and then throwing with an overarm throw to score a basket. They will enjoy practising this individually, keeping their own score. Decisions about the amount of strength to achieve the correct height and the placing of the hand on the ball to achieve the correct direction are all important movement learning experiences.

Bouncing and catching

- Bouncing should be practised individually, 'on the spot' first, then with the children walking slowly – aware of others moving around them. Once this is mastered, the speed can be increased.
- In twos facing one another, the children bounce and catch. Those who find this difficult may find it helpful to say the words as they try. It can be helpful to put a line or cross on the floor to show where the ball should bounce. The distance and speed can be increased once the pattern is established. Varying the direction of the bounce slightly so that the receiver has to anticipate where, when and how to move is a fun progression which helps tracking.
- In a small circle, bouncing the ball across the space. This is good practice for children who find it difficult to estimate the amount of strength they will need. It also helps visual tracking.

Throwing and catching

- Individually throwing a ball into the air and catching it. Although the trajectory of the ball is different from that needed in most games, the children are in charge of the distance and the pace. The teaching points should emphasise the hand action – a single hand action followed immediately by making a 'basket' which has to go right underneath the falling ball.
- In twos sympathetically passing the ball back and forward. It is fun if a target is set: who can pass the ball five times without dropping it? However, this shouldn't be done against the clock till the skill is mastered or the throw will be rushed and ineffective. Teachers should check the stance, i.e. opposite foot to the throwing hand forward, for if the children stand square on to the direction of throw, the action becomes a poke rather than a smooth, swinging underarm action.
- Mini-game – Donkey in the Middle. This game really needs an overarm throwing action so needs different skills from the

underarm throw. The stance is the same – the arm action changes so that the hand comes above shoulder level. Foam balls travel slowly and are good for early practices. Volleyballs are best because although they look like the real thing, they are lighter than a basketball and don't hurt.

And so there are many fun ways to help children improve their movements. Building activities so that balance, rhythm, direction and timing demands gradually increase helps children to become coordinated, efficient and effective movers in a variety of environments. Teachers will know they have succeeded, that all the planning and preparation was worthwhile, when their children say, 'Look at me, I can do it too!' (Photo 16).

Photo 16 Look at me, I can do it too!

Developmental norms

	Locomotor patterns	Non-locomotor patterns	Manipulative skills
1 month		Can lift head from lying on front	Can retain object placed in hand
3–4 months		Stepping reflex pattern	Plays with hands as first toy
5 months	Rolls over from back	Holds head and shoulders erect when sitting	Stretching out to grasp objects
6–8 months		Sitting unsupported; pulling up to stand	Reaching accurately; grasping; letting go
9 months	Crawling; climbing up stairs	Supports cup/bottle; copes with finger food	Transfers objects from one hand to another
10 months	Walks around furniture	Bends to pick up object and stands again with one hand support	Makes toys work
1 year	Walks unsteadily with feet apart and arms outstretched to balance	Will start games such as peek-a-boo	Plays with building bricks and other toys; pulls off socks, shoes
2 years	Walks well, learning to run; climbs on toys and furniture	Dismantles everything; enjoys simple wooden lift out puzzles	Builds towers; pours water from one jug to another
2–3 years	Can ride tricycle; climbs up and down stairs – both feet on each step; walks on tiptoe	Enjoys jigsaws, painting, gluing	Can lift heavier objects with some control; takes clothes off; puts on pants, T-shirt
3–4 years	Learning to hop and balance	Can catch large ball; can release objects more easily now	Can draw circle; can button cardigan or coat
5 years	Can walk, run, skip and hop, even cycle and swim	Enjoys 'bunny jumps' and balancing activities	Can form letters and numbers; hits ball with bat; can tie shoes (5+)

Age-related development of movement patterns

Summary notes on dyspraxia

A difficulty in planning and carrying out a sequence of organised, coordinated movements with associated difficulties with perception and thought.

Dyspraxia

Bright orally but with poor performance skills, results in difficulty with fine motor skills such as writing which requires control, many everyday coping skills, e.g. tying laces, pouring, getting dressed, and gross motor skills such as running, crawling. Coordination e.g. kicking a ball very difficult. Children don't understand what is wrong – frustration may lead to unacceptable behaviour. Often this is treated without finding the root cause.

Children

Many signs, often floppiness – poor muscle control around a joint; may be verbal dyspraxia making articulation problematic. Probably did not crawl and so missed important balance and perceptual learning (direction and distance) and opportunities to practise segmented coordinated movements. Poor body awareness and sense of body boundary, therefore bumping and bruising results.

Signs

The children look just the same as others. They have a 'hidden handicap' (Kirby 1999), therefore they are often denied understanding. Condition does not improve with maturation alone.

Appearance

Between 8 and 10 per cent This means that there will be children with some degree of dyspraxia in every class. Many more boys than girls (four to one), but girls tend to be more severely affected.

Numbers

No gross neurological deficit such as cerebral palsy, but almost certainly links with Asperger Syndrome, dyslexia, ADHD. May have poorly integrated reflexes.

Links

Perceptual difficulties	Inaccurate information from the senses leads to uncoordinated movement.
Visual	Poor tracking, therefore copying from the board into a jotter very difficult. May not be able to cut out visual distractors so concentration affected.
Kinaesthetic	Poor body and spatial awareness. Poor sense of body boundary. Judging distances faulty, therefore clumsiness.
Vestibular	Poor balance, can't ride a bike without stabilisers till long after peers.
Proprioceptive	Nerve endings in muscles and joints don't relay place information accurately, therefore movement hesitant. Children have to see rather than sense where their body parts are.
Anecdotal	Children say: 'No one will let me play. It's not fair.' 'Why can't I skate too?' 'I'm trying. I know what I want my hands to do. I see it in my brain but my hands just won't do it.' 'Mum, there's another party and I'm not invited again. Why not?'
Teachers	Don't offer rewards: these children are already trying as hard as they can. Reduce the number of sums etc. and avoid giving homework; the children are too tired, and as many are bright, it may be unnecessary. Parents have enough problems without struggling with schoolwork at home.

Books on dyspraxia are listed in the Bibliography

Bibliography

Ayres, J. A. (1972) *Sensory Integration and Learning Disorders*. Los Angeles: Western Psychological Services.

Blythe, P. (1992) 'A physical approach to resolving learning difficulties', paper presented at the Fourth European Conference of Neuro-developmental Delay in Children, Chester.

Caan, W. (1998) Foreword, in Portwood, M., *Developmental Dyspraxia, Identification and Intervention: A Manual for Parents and Professionals*, 2nd edn. London: David Fulton Publishers.

Chesson R. *et al.* (1990) *The Child with Motor/Learning Difficulties*. Aberdeen: Royal Aberdeen Children's Hospital.

Cotrell, S. (1992) 'The effects of obstetric problems on neuro-developmental delay', paper presented at the Fourth European Conference on Developmental Delay, March.

DfEE (2000) *Curriculum Guidance for the Foundation Stage*. London: Qualifications and Curriculum Authority.

Dighe, A. and Kettles, G. (1996) 'Developmental dyspraxia: an overview', in Reid, G. (ed.) *Dimensions of Dyslexia*, vol. 2. Edinburgh: Moray House Institute.

Dobie, S. (1996) 'Perceptual-motor and neuro-developmental dimensions', in Reid, G. (ed.) *Dimensions of Dyslexia*, vol. 2. Edinburgh: Moray House Institute.

Dussart, G. (1994) 'Identifying the clumsy child in school: an exploratory study', *British Journal of Special Education* 21(2).

Dyspraxia Foundation (1999) *Praxis makes Perfect*. Hitchin, Herts: Dyspraxia Foundation.

Keen, D. (2001) 'Looking at casuality, prevalence and comorbidity? Paper presented at the Durham conference on dyspraxia, March.

Kirby, A. (1999) *Dyspraxia: The Hidden Handicap*. London: Souvenir Press.

Losse, A. *et al.* (1991) 'Clumsiness in children: do they grow out of it? A 10 year study', *Developmental Medicine and Child Neurology* **33**, 55–68.

Macintyre, C. (1998) 'Helping children with movement difficulties', *Education 3–13* **26**(1).

Macintyre, C. (2000) *Dyspraxia in the Early Years*. London: David Fulton Publishers.

Macintyre, C. (2001a) *Dyspraxia 5–11*. London: David Fulton Publishers.

Macintyre, C. (2001b) *Enhancing Learning through Play*. London: David Fulton Publishers.

Portwood, M. (1999) *Developmental Dyspraxia, Identification and Intervention: A Manual for Parents and Professionals*, 2nd edn. London: David Fulton Publishers.

Rasmussen, A. *et al.* (1983) 'Perceptual motor and attentional deficits in 7-year-old children: neurological and neuro-developmental aspects', *Developmental Medicine and Child Neurology* **25**.

Ripley, K. *et al.* (1997) *Dyspraxia: A Guide for Teachers and Parents*. London: David Fulton Publishers.

Scottish Office Education and Industry Department (SOEID) (1992) *Curriculum and Assessment Guidelines: Expressive Arts 5–14*. Edinburgh: Scottish Office.

Sugden, D. A. and Henderson, S. E. (1994) 'Help with movement', *Special Children 75: Back to Basics 13.*

Index

coordinated movement 1, 3, 5, 6, 25–6, 29, 59, 60, 74, 80, 83–4
efficient and effective movement 1, 4, 12, 18, 34, 80

National guidelines (5–14) 61

observation schedules 6, 49–50
circuits 47, 51
sticky labels 46
time sampling 54
video recording 7, 54, 55

parental responses 19, 54–5, 57
involvement 48, 50, 56, 58, 84
pencil grips 29
percussion 44, 48–9, 60
piano, playing the 29
pincer grip activities 31
primitive reflexes 10
prone kneeling 20, 26
proprioceptive sense 35, 84

rhymes 9, 37, 60, 72
rolling 26, 27–8, 30, 36, 40, 68
running 3, 6, 10, 12–13, 16, 17–19, 79, 83

safety 1, 27, 37, 46–7, 75–6
Scottish Office Education and Industry Department 61
sensory integration 34, 45
sensory perception 7, 34, 43, 83
sensory-motor pathway 34
sequencing activities 4, 9, 31, 42
skipping 10, 22–4, 72, 78
spatial awareness 11, 16, 31, 34–5, 38, 47, 59, 63, 70
stability 10, 63
standing 11, 12
strength 28–9 30, 38

tactile sense 44–5
throwing 10, 17, 28, 78–9
touching/supporting children 6, 7, 48, 58–9
tracking 28, 29, 39, 78–9, 84
transfer of learning 60
transitions 25, 27, 42

vestibular sense 40, 84
visual sense 28, 31, 39, 41, 42, 43, 79

walking 10, 12–14, 16, 17
writing 1, 3, 29, 30, 42, 55, 83